Leading a School Budget Review

Julie Cordiner & Nikola Flint

First published in Great Britain in 2018
by School Financial Success Publications
Copyright © 2018 Julie Cordiner & Nikola Flint

ISBN: 0995590214
ISBN-13: 978-0995590212

To our families, especially the younger generations.

Inspiring School Financial Success to support schools today

for a brighter future tomorrow.

CONTENTS

PREFACE

Introduction

If you're reading this book, it is likely that you are either leading a budget review yourself or you are expecting someone else to. Whatever your purpose, you will learn why budget reviews are needed, how they are carried out and what they can achieve, all presented in an easy to understand and logical format. You will deepen your understanding of influencing factors, related roles and responsibilities and the importance of effective change management for a review to be successful.

The best thing is, it's not all theory. Practical advice for implementation and relevant examples of scenarios make it easy for you to lead your own budget review, or guide someone else to do so.

Why is a budget review necessary?

Schools are responsible for public money, and with that responsibility comes accountability. Achieving value for money (VfM) is crucial for both the school's financial health and positive outcomes for pupils. Promoting VfM is therefore a professional and moral responsibility for all school staff, and especially for those leaders who are responsible for financial management in schools.

The current financial climate in education is challenging and uncertain. The implementation of a National Funding Formula (NFF) is at last becoming a reality, but the government can only make information available for the first two years, 2018/19 and 2019/20, and the ultimate impact on school budgets will still depend on local decisions. Understanding the national context of school funding reform is important, if you are to ensure your budget is responsive to changes in the overall amount of money you are likely to have in the coming years.

Despite the government's announcement in July 2017 that there would be enough funding in the system to achieve an increase of at least 0.5% per pupil for every school, the guidance to local authorities for 2018/19 makes it clear that schools can still experience a reduction in funding of up to 1.5% per pupil per year. This can happen where there are changes made to the local formula and/or where the local authority does not receive sufficient funding for some costs that sit outside the NFF. All schools are experiencing increasing costs, particularly in relation to staffing, and there is a question mark over whether even those gaining from the NFF will receive sufficient to cover cost pressures.

The National Audit Office report 'Financial Sustainability of Schools', published in December 2016, cited an 8.0% real-terms reduction in per-pupil funding for mainstream schools between 2014-15 and 2019-20 due to cost pressures. The use of the word 'real-terms' involves a comparison with actual costs, i.e. not only extra pupils but also inflation and other necessary increases in expenditure (such as the Apprenticeship Levy).

The NAO report highlighted the DfE's estimate that savings of £3 billion need to be made by mainstream schools by 2019-20 to counteract these cost pressures. By 2014/15, the proportion of secondary academies and maintained schools spending more than their income had risen rapidly, reaching 60%, and for primary LA maintained schools the figure was around a third. It is therefore clear that current funding is already insufficient to support many schools' priorities.

Some schools may have depleted their reserves in recent years, or may already have a deficit. The danger is that positive outcomes are built on unsustainable levels of spending, and when action has to be taken, there could be a risk to the standards that the school has achieved. While Ofsted focuses on the use of Pupil Premium and other specific grants, inspectors pay little attention to the use of the most significant element of a school's funding, their budget share (or General Annual Grant for academies). Every school needs to be its own watchdog, to ensure that funding is used wisely.

It is difficult to make a general assessment of whether the funding provided by DfE in future will cover ongoing cost pressures, as it depends on each school's starting point and the way in which the NFF impacts on them. As most of the increased need to spend relates to the cost of employing staff, schools spending a higher than average proportion of their budget on staffing are likely to find it more difficult to manage.

Some local formulae may replicate the NFF in capping gains at 3% per pupil per year for 2018/19 and 2019/20, so schools that are due to gain from the new formula might not receive all of the benefit immediately. There could also be an impact on mainstream schools in areas which are only receiving a minimal increase in High Needs funding, either because money originally intended for school budgets might have to be transferred to cover High Needs pressures, or because LAs may look to place more children with SEND in mainstream schools rather than in specialist provision.

A budget review is therefore likely to be an important tool in supporting a school's future financial success; for some schools it may make the difference between surviving and thriving.

The purpose of a budget review is to reduce areas of waste and promote VfM across the many different aspects of school life. Undertaken properly, it will support a review of the school's priorities, ensuring adequate funding is available to make those priorities happen.

For schools wanting to avoid or minimise staffing reductions which could impact negatively on pupil outcomes, our focus on review of non-pay budgets offers alternative solutions for cost reductions. Where this is insufficient to address the school's financial problems, we also offer advice on reviewing staffing. We will be offering a future publication sharing our expertise on developing an income strategy, but this book helps you to consider your existing income generation activity and provides guidance to ensure you are getting the best out of the opportunities available to you.

Your completed budget review will provide assurance that everything is being done in your school to secure a sustainable budget, ensuring that governors, funding bodies, external auditors and others with an interest in the school's viability can have confidence in the school's leadership.

Who leads it?

In a school with a School Business Leader, it would make sense for that person to take the lead in a budget review. This role may have several different titles, such as School Business Manager, Bursar, Finance Manager, Director of Finance etc. We use the generic term School Business Leader to refer to the lead person in the school business management profession.

The very nature of this person's role makes it more likely that they have the necessary information to hand, and the skills needed, to undertake the review successfully. However, a budget review can be led by any school leader who is allocated this responsibility. This guide supports all school leaders to lead a budget review logically, systematically and creatively to support ongoing school improvement and future financial success.

What is the focus?

A budget review aims to streamline the use of resources across all areas of the budget to promote a value for money culture among staff and stakeholders.

This guide, 'Leading a School Budget Review', focuses on the two key expenditure sections of a school budget in turn: pay budgets and non-pay budgets. Income generation will also be examined, as a means of supporting your school's financial sustainability.

Pay budgets make up the biggest proportion of expenditure in any school budget. Critical to the school's overall success is the ability to match the staffing structure to the needs of the school in line with the school's priorities, ensuring staff are in the right roles, in the right places, at the right times. In addition, matching the staffing structure and pay budgets to the available funding and deploying staff in a way that promotes VfM is a crucial element of your budget review and your school's future financial sustainability.

A school can have outstanding results, but if they are built on small class sizes and high teaching costs that are causing a massive overspend, it may not be possible to sustain standards in the long term, especially if a recovery plan requires major staffing reductions. The balance between these competing demands is a key focus of your budget review and the first step to truly achieving the value for money culture you are striving for.

Non-pay budgets are equally important. Although they make up a smaller overall proportion of the budget, this is still a substantial amount of money and there are significant savings to be made in these areas. You may be confident that your pay budgets represent VfM, yet you might still need to find savings. Reviewing your non-pay budgets may mitigate the need for staffing reductions which are likely to be considered undesirable and may impact negatively on pupil outcomes.

Even if you do not have a pressing need for savings, review of these budgets is important for school financial health. Waste may be reduced and unnecessary spending in one area could be re-allocated, resulting in a positive impact on the outcomes of your pupils.

Many schools have existing income opportunities. It is extremely important to ensure that the proper controls are in place to ensure accounting compliance, develop robust policy and procedure and maximise those opportunities. Income generation can act as a saving in your budget or can generate income to be redeployed to invest in school improvement strategies or resources. Either way, it can be a key factor for schools in securing financial sustainability.

How will a budget review help you and your school?

A budget review provides strong and robust evidence for quality assurance by the Headteacher and governors as well as for external review such as audit, the local authority (LA), the Education & Skills Funding Agency (ESFA) which carries out accountability monitoring for the Department for Education (DfE), and Ofsted.

It also gives others confidence in your ability to be proactive in responding to financial challenges and to secure a viable future for the school. It may support you to achieve your appraisal or performance objectives and provide a platform to support your leadership development and potentially your future career progression.

Using this book

This book is divided into four parts:

Part 1 describes a clear, easy to understand process for leading a budget review. It offers advice on how to approach this difficult and complex task in a way that gets staff buy-in, secures results and promotes continuous school improvement.

Part 2 details the remit of the teams undertaking the budget review, with a focus on managing cultural and procedural change and detailed action planning.

Part 3 provides a step by step guide to the review of some key budget areas, prompting self-reflection and offering practical advice which can be interpreted in your own context.

Part 4 advises you on finalising your review with particular emphasis on forecasting and monitoring the impact of your review and keeping stakeholders informed.

Throughout all parts a common-sense approach to achieving VfM is shared, to enable you to impact positively on your whole school systems, processes, procedures and, importantly, your school culture.

Part 1: Role of the Budget Review Leader

1 OVERVIEW OF THE ROLE

Planning the review

As the budget review leader, you are responsible for planning the review, establishing the wider leadership of it and securing the resources to carry it out successfully. This can be coordinated in a strategic action plan.

To be able to complete your strategic action plan, you need to understand your budget. This will help you to self-assess your school's position in relation to pay budgets and identify non-pay budget areas for review. All of this information will feed back into your strategic action plan.

There are also quick wins to your budget review, such as a review of your financial procedures and longer-term arrangements, for example collaboration and strengthening partnerships.

Part 1 considers each of these areas in turn. It's a good idea to read all of Part 1 before tackling your strategic action plan for your budget review, as key information throughout this section will support you to develop a thorough and rigorous plan.

The wider leadership of the budget review requires you to lead teams effectively, ensuring appropriate skill sets are focused in the right areas and that the budget review stays on track throughout. One of the most important and most challenging aspects of the budget review leader role is to manage change, potentially adopting a range of techniques to suit the many different circumstances of your overall budget review. These aspects are considered in detail in Part 2.

Stages of the strategic action plan

The strategic action plan is a working document with five key stages:
- Clarify objectives
- Form teams
- Identify timelines
- Identify resources
- Implementation and monitoring

You will recognise the process from your school development planning, which should include the priority for improvement, who is responsible, by when, at what cost and how it will be monitored. You may refer to each heading slightly differently but the principle is the same.

Clarify Objectives

<u>Overarching objective</u>

Think of your budget review strategic action plan as an offshoot of your school development plan (SDP). You will need an introduction which describes your overarching objective, setting the context for the whole review.

What is your overarching objective?

- Are you responding to a potential loss of funding because of changes in rolls or the impact of school funding reforms, which might not fully cover cost pressures?
- Do you have an existing deficit that needs to be addressed, or a loan that needs to be repaid, in which case your budget review will be part of your recovery plan?
- Do you need to assure stakeholders that the school is financially viable going forward? Stakeholders might include governors, the LA, the Education and Skills Funding Agency (ESFA) or other schools that you are potentially looking to work with in either formal or informal collaboration.
- Perhaps you are faced with falling rolls or the threat of school reorganisation.
- You might have just received a poor Ofsted judgement and need to re-allocate budgets to allow significant spending on school improvement strategies.
- Are you looking to review the school's priorities, perhaps as part of a driver for change, for example to provide new senior leadership capacity, and need to ensure there is adequate funding available to make priorities happen?
- Are you considering a reduction in staffing (perhaps for one of the reasons already described above) but want to avoid any negative impact on pupil outcomes by focusing your review on non-pay budgets, offering alternative solutions for cost reductions?
- Or you may simply want to ensure that you are providing value for money education, reducing waste and being as prepared as possible for the uncertainties of future school funding and the pressures of increasing costs.

Reporting the outcomes

In the introduction to your strategic action plan, you will need to identify to whom you are planning to report the outcomes. This will depend on what your overarching objective is. You may produce an internal document that will only be reported to governors. Alternatively, the budget review may form part of a deficit recovery plan or repayment plans for an existing loan, in which case it will need to be reported to the LA or ESFA.

Areas of priority

As with a school development plan, there will be different areas of priority to tackle. In this context, these are the different budget areas that you are planning to review. Which areas of the budget are you planning to tackle and why? You may already be aware that you have areas of overspending or know that you are not making the most of your income opportunities. You may have used benchmarking tools which have highlighted that you have a high spend per pupil in some areas of your budget. If valid reasons for this cannot be identified, then a budget review of this area is a good idea, to reduce waste, measure impact on outcomes and achieve VfM. Read on in this section to help you identify your key areas of priority.

Objectives for priority areas

Once established, each priority area of the budget will require its own set of specific objectives and related actions. Imagine you have split your overall school development plan into sections, perhaps relating to teaching and learning or personal development, behaviour and welfare as two examples. These sections would each require their own objectives and associated actions with identified resourcing, timelines and monitoring. Your priority budget areas in your review are, in effect, these sections.

As a starting point, you may decide to work through each section identifying objectives and actions on your own. However, it is more likely and advisable that you give the team who will be carrying out the actions the opportunity to be involved in formulating the objectives and actions in the first place. We will expand on this later.

Special considerations

Consider if there are any special considerations for each priority area. For example, when considering pay budgets, you may know the staff structure you currently have in place is not ideal, but there may be restrictions on any immediate change such as TUPE regulations - Transfer of Undertakings (Protection of Employment) - from an academy conversion, which provide certain entitlements for staff transferring between employers.

For non-pay budgets, a special consideration might be that you are tied into a lease agreement, perhaps for accommodation or equipment. You will need to understand and abide by the terms and conditions of the lease when planning to introduce any changes, to ensure you are not faced with any penalty charges. Depending on the change you want to make, it may sometimes be worth paying to be released from the contract, but you need to consider the payback period, i.e. how long it will take for savings to outstrip the penalty charge.

Success criteria

The success criteria define how you will know that you have achieved your objective. You should set out the criteria in your introduction to the overall plan, to show how you will measure your success against your overarching objective.

As an example, if your objective is to clear an existing deficit, your success criteria could include the school achieving a balanced budget in the next financial year with a deficit recovery plan fully implemented, the deficit cleared and the funding received in each financial year covering all costs required to meet the school's priorities. Achieving a reserves target would be another criterion, or generating enough savings to fund an important project for improved outcomes.

You will also need success criteria for each of your objectives within priority areas. A good example in this context is to consider if there are any target savings for individual priority areas at this point. Do you know you need to save 30% of the existing budget, for example? What is this in monetary terms? It helps to be specific, as this information will help you in the monitoring stages later. Perhaps you need to review one area of the budget to make savings which will release funding to be used for another initiative. Provide the detail of what is needed for the new initiative to be successful.

Your success criteria will form the basis for measuring whether your overall budget review has been successful. Think carefully about what is realistic and achievable, as well as what your overarching objective demands from the budget review.

Form teams

Regardless of school size or set-up, the involvement of other staff in your budget review is critical to its immediate and sustained success. Inevitably, there will be some parts of your budget review which require cultural change to bring about financial efficiency.

Cultural change is achieved by altering the behaviour of the people within the community. In the case of a school, this is primarily its staff and pupils, with some focus on other stakeholders such as governors, parents and partners. To achieve staff buy-in as the main driver for cultural change, the wider staff body needs to see that representatives from key teams have been involved in the process for change from the outset.

This promotes a feeling of ownership amongst staff as well as a confidence that their views are being considered and the process is being carried out 'with them' and not done 'to them'. This is basic change management and a common-sense approach for most school leaders, but it is important to refer to it here as an important reminder.

It's easy to see why leaders can get caught out when time is limited and all staff are busy. Sometimes projects get rushed through without an adequate level of staff involvement and shortcuts are taken. Whilst some cracks can be smoothed over along the way, the overall process will be a bumpy ride at best. At worst, the project will fail if staff are not given the opportunity or encouragement to get on board.

In forming teams to support a budget review exercise, you will need to identify how much capacity you think is needed for each priority budget area. Ask yourself these questions as a checklist for each area:

✓ Will the priority area be tackled by you alone, by you with support from other staff, or by others with your line management?

✓ If a team is needed, who are the key individuals in your school who you think need to be involved?

✓ Do you think that the number of people involved is appropriate (too few and you risk not being able to achieve objectives, too many and you are not being efficient)?

✓ If you have too few, are there any other staff who have the capacity and skills to provide support?

✓ Can the anticipated workload be subsumed in the normal working day of the team members?

✓ Can time together be easily achieved: matched time, and space to work?

✓ Who is the team leader for this priority budget area?

✓ Do any team members have any training needs in relation to the budget review? What are they? Can these training needs be met easily, at an acceptable cost and within a required timeframe?

✓ How will teams report their progress back to you and how frequently?

As more people become involved in the review, the more critical your communication skills become, as the budget review leader. Ensure your messages are clear, concise, relevant and recorded. We talk about communication in greater detail towards the end of the book.

Identify timelines

It is important to identify a timeline for your overall budget review, and for each area within it, from the outset. As with a school development plan, if you do not create an end point, there is a danger that priorities you identify at the beginning may be allowed to run and run without any real progress or conclusion.

Your timelines need to be realistically set, considering the capacity and resources available to undertake the review. But ultimately it is the budget review's over-arching objective which will drive your timeline. As the budget review leader, you need to marry the staffing capacity and resources with the desired timeline to ensure the best possible chances of overall success.

Consider your over-arching objectives and ask yourself the following questions to help you to determine timelines across your review:

- Is there a target date for overall completion driven by **external** factors such as:
    - a deficit recovery plan?
    - repayment of an existing loan?
    - other information required by your LA, the ESFA or DfE?
    - partners or potential partners requiring assurances on the school's future financial viability/sustainability?
    - re-allocation of budgets to enable significant spending on school improvement strategies following a poor Ofsted judgement?
- Is there a target date for overall completion driven by **internal** factors such as:
    - financial pressures revealed in future financial forecasts?
    - falling rolls?
    - the need to avoid staffing reductions? Perhaps the review needs to be completed before a final deadline for beginning a staff review consultation, so you know you can achieve redundancies by the end of the academic year, if insufficient financial savings are found in other parts of the review.

We have included a high-level example of a timeline for staff review consultation in Appendix 1. Please note that consultation periods and notice pay can vary, depending on the organisation and the individuals involved. The example we have given is for demonstration purposes only.

- Are you undertaking the review solely to improve your value for money culture?

If the last question fits your situation you will find there is much less pressure on you for a quick turnaround. However, the sooner the review is complete, the sooner waste is reduced and financial savings can be made.

It is good practice to identify some quick wins as well as long term gains within the planning stages of your review.

Quick wins

Quick wins are visible improvements that are widely perceived as positive amongst your key stakeholders. They should have immediate benefit and be delivered quickly after your review begins. They might not have deep or long-term impact, but they help to get buy-in at the beginning and convince people that the review as a whole is a good thing and worth investing in. Quick wins are particularly important in sparking cultural change and getting people on board.

An example of a quick win in a budget review might be a price reduction for an expensive resource or service for one year that enables funding to be released to another budget area where impact is widely visible. Benefits might be achieved from the appointment of a temporary additional member of staff or an apprentice, with a specific focus where you know staff and students will see an immediate positive impact.

Another quick win might be the identification of historic practices or processes that use a lot of resources but don't deliver any benefits. It is easy for staff to do things 'because we've always done it this way', but asking the staff themselves to pull apart a process and analyse why they do it can bring some creative ideas about different approaches and relieve them from wasting time on pointless tasks.

There might be a procedural quick win with your income streams. For example, are you applying procedures to avoid bad debts so that the income you plan to generate is actually collected?

Long-term gains

Long-term gains achieve the initial objectives and sustain benefit over a longer period. These can be harder to achieve, but without them your budget review will miss the opportunity to address the key issue of your school's financial sustainability. Long-term gains, in the context of a school budget review, are often reliant on changes in people's behaviour. They are about embedding these behavioural changes as a way of life within your school to truly achieve the VfM culture you are striving for.

An example of a long-term gain in a budget review might be an overhaul of the way printing and photocopying is undertaken, moving towards better use of digital communication, reducing unnecessary waste and significantly reducing costs year on year.

Sometimes gains can only be achieved in the longer term, because of restrictions such as the length of contracts for services, or because they require other partners to agree to change their practices.

To help you to ensure you can work within the timelines you have identified, you will need to:

- identify reporting deadlines and ensure these are effectively communicated;
- ensure there are regular progress updates and follow-up actions to minimise the risk of delayed outcomes;
- communicate unavoidable changes to your timeline to relevant parties, so you can manage expectations.

Identify resources

Next you will need to identify any resources you require to enable your budget review to be carried out effectively. Just like the school development plan, if adequate resources are not allocated to each objective then the plan simply becomes a wish list and the likelihood of all, or any part, of it being achieved is significantly diminished.

You probably won't want to be spending a lot of money on the review, simply by the nature of the task you are undertaking. However, there may be priority budget areas which require some investment to achieve long term gains. For example, capital investment in new reprographics/printing machinery, or revenue investment in a new lease agreement to upgrade this machinery, may promise a better quality of service, cheaper cost per copy and lower regular spending on printing and photocopying.

You need to be clear about what resources are available at the beginning of the review before it goes ahead, and you should also make sure anyone involved understands this. Should opportunities arise for more significant 'spend to save' proposals, these should be reviewed on a case by case basis with a full risk assessment of the investment to be made against potential savings over time.

Remember, even if a proposal looks like a good idea, you may simply not have the funds to make it happen. Can you be sure that the savings you are being promised will come to fruition? You will need to call on some key leadership skills and characteristics to make critical decisions in these situations, and allow your team to play to its strengths, enabling members of staff to contribute to the decision-making process. The key skills and characteristics you will need across your team include creativity, determination, prudence, risk-assessment and analytical skills.

The most important thing to remember is not to lose sight of your objectives: your over-arching objective and the objectives within each priority budget area. The decisions you make need to be in line with these objectives and must not jeopardise the school's position.

The main resource you will need for your budget review is people's time, which hopefully entails a re-focusing of work and priorities rather than any significant addition.

Implementation and monitoring

The final key area of your strategic action plan is implementation and monitoring.

We have already touched on some of the ways this can happen, but it is important to bring it together and think about this key part of your planning process.

Who will have responsibility for monitoring progress against each action point? Have you ensured that the person monitoring the work is not the person who is doing the work? There is an obvious conflict if it is the same person, making the monitoring process weak and less effective.

Are all teams clear on their roles, responsibilities for monitoring progress and the mechanism for reporting back to you as the leader? Do your key staff know what action to take if staff they are monitoring don't act as they should or miss deadlines? Will this be reported to you? Are you clear on how you will deal with it at that point?

In the context of a budget review, a key point in monitoring progress is to link the review back to the whole school budget monitoring process. This could involve making comparisons against monthly reports of a particular budget area to identify if expected savings are being made as anticipated. The person carrying out the budget review may not be the person responsible for preparing monthly budget reports, so you need to ensure that this crossover is appropriate, purposeful and useful.

This leads us to the importance of understanding your budget before you embark on developing your budget review strategic action plan.

2 UNDERSTAND YOUR BUDGET

Budget knowledge

If you are the school business leader in your school, you are likely to know your budget inside out, back to front and upside down, which puts you in a great position to carry out the review. If you are not, you may need to undertake some pre-work to develop a deeper understanding than you currently have. This will pay off throughout your review and is absolutely essential if you want your review to be a success.

Don't be put off if you feel you are starting from far back in the field. The advantage you have is a fresh set of eyes and the art of the innocent question, both techniques that can open up a whole world of opportunity potentially missed by those that work with the budget on a regular basis.

Budget format and headings

You need to understand what your budget looks like for the type of school you are. Different types of school have different budget formats, i.e. LA maintained or an academy, so you should familiarise yourself with each of the budget headings.

Understand what each budget heading means and what types of expenditure should be posted there. Importantly, you need to understand the difference between different categories of budget heading: pay, pay related, non-pay and income budgets.

As well as these 'subjective' headings, you will be conscious of more functional areas, related to particular aspects of your school's activities. Examples might be school improvement initiatives for particular subjects across the school or under-performing groups of pupils, special educational needs and disabilities (SEND), behaviour and attendance, pupil well-being, pastoral activities and so on.

Spending on these functional areas does not appear in the formal financial accounting reports but you can build plans for them in a management accounting sense. They are likely to appear in your school development plan. We will show you some examples of how to review these areas in a future chapter.

Another distinction you will need to make is between revenue expenditure (ongoing) and capital expenditure (usually higher cost, one-off expenditure related to building projects or major equipment purchases). Capital expenditure will be in the form of devolved capital allocations which you must use for defined purposes; your funding body will advise on any minimum thresholds for expenditure to count as capital. It is possible to use revenue funding to make an additional contribution to a capital project, but it is not possible for schools to convert capital funding into revenue.

However, if you are spending significant sums from your revenue budget on IT equipment or refurbishment, there could be an opportunity to re-classify it as capital expenditure, subject of course to the availability of capital funding to cover it. This will provide a saving to your annual budget.

Make sure you understand the difference between funding and income. Funding is the money allocated to you from your funding body, such as your budget share/General Annual Grant or pupil premium grants. Income is generated directly by the school, a common example being for school lettings.

Deep analysis

Now you have an understanding of the overall scope of your budget, you need to start to dig down into each area within it to get a feel of issues, patterns, trends and unusual items.

The first question to ask is whether you are maximising your funding. Is your census data accurate? This influences the majority of your school budget share or General Annual Grant funding. Records of nursery pupils are essential for attracting early years funding. Are you submitting information when requested by the local authority, for example in relation to pupils with SEND, which could yield extra money?

Do you qualify for any discretionary funds held by the local authority such as Temporary Falling Rolls funds, Growth Fund, Schools in Financial Difficulty funding or any school improvement initiatives? Academies are also eligible for the first three of these (if they exist). There could be some in-kind support available if you are part of a local Trust or MAT, or from a

Teaching School Alliance, health body or voluntary sector organisation working on an area of need that is relevant to your pupils, such as mental health or physical health. There are specific grants available from the Education & Skills Funding Agency (ESFA) for academies, such as a post-opening grant.

Schools will have many examples of unusual items. The trick in the deep analysis is to identify which items are unusual for your school context. For example, you may find that your school spends a significant amount on hire of vehicles. This may be entirely justifiable if you hire vehicles for school trips and events, or if your pupil profile and school context is such that you support individual pupils with transport to and from school at your expense. A high spend in this budget area may not be so desirable if you do not employ these strategies. The deep analysis will allow you to identify the reasons for the spend and consider if these are justified or not.

A high spend on IT equipment over the course of the year may be understandable if you are aware of a significant planned IT refresh programme. It may be less desirable and worthy of further investigation and review if such a roll out was unplanned and uncoordinated. Have individual departments purchased equipment with no strategic planning? What are the implications?

For income headings, make sure you have a clear understanding of the transactions that sit behind each one and what they relate to. Are they categorised in a logical manner? Is it clear where income and expenditure in the budget relate to each other, perhaps shown as separate management accounts?

It is a useful exercise at this point to check the accuracy of posting in the chart of accounts. If items are recorded in the wrong areas, this will skew the financial information you are looking at and potentially take you down the wrong path for your review. You may check this yourself or you may work with other colleagues.

Make sure you record your findings in an organised way for your review so that you can refer back to them with ease at any time.

Surpluses and deficits

You need to consider whether your school has any surplus balances, including surpluses that have built up over time or anticipated balances in the current financial year. How and why have these surpluses come about? Are there any existing plans for their use that you need to be aware of? Have you been challenged by your LA or the ESFA if they regard the level of balances as excessive?

If your school has a deficit, or anticipated deficit, you will no doubt be aware of this; it is likely to be a key reason for your budget review. What is your planned timescale, identified in your recovery plan, for getting back into balance? Your review will need to be built around the requirements imposed by your funding body and you will need to keep these in mind throughout your review.

Budget link to School Development Plan (SDP)

The relationship between your budget and your SDP is extremely important. We have already touched on why it is crucial for an SDP to have sufficient resource allocated to each priority area, to ensure that the plan is affordable. It is also vital to ensure that this resource allocation is reflected in your budget.

For your budget review, you need to understand which areas of the budget relate to particular priorities on your SDP and be clear that the relevant areas are linked together, with no discrepancies or omissions on either side. The first book in this series, School Budget Mastery, includes a suggested template to map your costed SDP priorities to budget headings.

If you are reviewing an area of the budget and you introduce a strategy to reduce spending, how will it impact on the SDP? The pressure on schools to 'do more with less' could mean that you are reducing expenditure across several areas of the budget and that the priorities in the SDP need to remain in place. If this is the case, do these priorities need to be reviewed to establish more creative ways of achieving them with less funding? Are there strong links between priorities that could be explored to find more efficient ways of delivering them, or of monitoring and evaluating their impact? You may need to be willing to make suggestions to colleagues on how this can be done.

Whilst you're not expected to be an expert in everyone else's specialist areas, you will need a solid understanding of the content of the SDP and the priorities within it. This will allow you to make realistic judgements regarding changes to funding allocations for different priority areas, if this is a possibility.

If there isn't an appropriate allocation of funding to every area of the SDP, does the SDP need to be amended, or does your budget review need to consider this and try to release funding to be allocated to those areas?

These two planning documents, the SDP and the budget, are inter-related and a sound understanding of both is essential for school leaders and essential to the success of your budget review.

3 UNDERSTAND VALUE FOR MONEY (VFM)

A Value for Money model

The most basic, yet most important, lesson for you in leading your budget review is to understand the principles of value for money (VfM) and to apply these principles throughout the review.

Overall, VfM is usually defined as ensuring the best possible outcomes are achieved for a given amount of money spent. A common approach is pictured below.

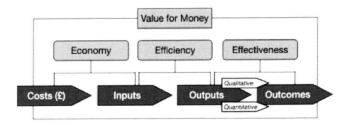

Economy is purely about the amount of money spent in order to create inputs, for example, the budget set aside to achieve a number of teaching staff in a school, what it costs to run your buildings, or the cost of educational resources. It is more concerned with how cheaply you can buy things, rather than what is achieved with them. **The economy stage is all about minimising the amount of money that goes towards your staffing plan, procurement strategy and individual contracts for resources or services** including cleaning, catering and so on. But you need to achieve the right balance between cost and quality, otherwise you may be wasting money on items that are not fit for purpose.

Efficiency is about how much output you get by using the inputs – what you do (the activities in your school) and who you reach (the different groups of pupils). Outputs are those results which are achieved immediately after implementing an activity. It is about how many pupils you teach with the staff provided, how many children get to go on educational visits, and how many pupils are entered for examinations from the exam fees budget. As well as quantitative measures, there can be qualitative aspects – the quality of teaching, an experienced specialist teacher for a specific area of the curriculum, or how long books and pens last.

Outputs are not the benefits or changes you achieve for your pupils; they are the interventions you make to bring about those achievements. Outputs are therefore not the same as outcomes. **The efficiency stage is all about achieving your curriculum plan to deliver education, and how you structure your school's operations using all available resources to maximise your pupils' entitlement to learning.**

Effectiveness is where outcomes become important. Outcomes represent the difference that the outputs have made, e.g. whether children succeed in their tests and examinations, whether children with EAL learn to speak English fluently so they can communicate effectively with their peers and with adults in order to learn, and whether pupils grow into confident adults, able to manage their own behaviour and take advantage of all the opportunities life presents. **The effectiveness stage is about your school improvement plan, and about what the pupils actually achieve with the teaching and guidance they have been given.**

Outcomes are so much more than a set of exam results demonstrating knowledge – they are about attitudes, skills, aspirations, motivations, and behaviours. Over a longer period, they are about building capability in decision making, social action, being a good citizen, and economic independence as an adult. All of these are integral components of daily teaching in the classroom and guidance in the playground and elsewhere, but many of them do not come to fruition until some time after the output (e.g. the teaching and pastoral guidance) is received. Of course, it's possible to see both positive and negative outcomes.

Make sure you always link outcomes to your priorities, otherwise you might be doing the wrong things incredibly well!

Budget review assessment – measuring resource allocation

Many education commentators say that there is no definitive research to prove that the amount of money spent by a school makes a difference to outcomes. The obvious answer to this is that it isn't what you spend, it's the way that you spend it. Two schools with a common profile of pupils and circumstances may receive the same amount of funding, but achieve different results with it because of the way they deploy their resources.

The link between efficient and effective resource allocation and student achievement is therefore clear. If a school spends its money on the right things, in the right amounts, at the right times, it stands the best possible chance of academic success and the best possible student outcomes. If it doesn't pay attention to these aspects, outcomes could be severely compromised by insufficient, inefficient or ineffective resourcing. So how do schools know if they are successful when it comes to resource allocation?

Is it simply enough to look at student performance data and assume that if a school is performing well, its resource allocation is a success? You might assume that would be the case, but things are not always that straightforward.

A school can achieve excellent outcomes, but if it is doing so with unaffordable levels of staffing and small class sizes, the performance is unlikely to be sustained in the long term. Without careful planning and linking of the budget and the school improvement plan, curriculum plan and staffing plan, any requirement to reduce spending could put outcomes at risk.

Another important issue is the level of school balances. Significant reserves may be held, with no specific plans to use them. This does not represent value for money or equitable resource allocation; funding is intended for the pupils currently in school. You should keep a reasonable operating surplus for unexpected cost pressures. But once that has been set aside, if you have certain groups that are under-performing, any excess reserves should be allocated to the relevant priorities in the improvement plan. It is also worth bearing in mind that MATs will generally set each school a reserve target, and also that maintained schools and academies can sometimes have restrictions on the value of reserves carried forward.

So, taking all of this into account, how do you know if you are allocating your school's resources well and how can this be measured?

The following ten sets of questions will support your school to make a professional judgement on its resource allocation and are a very useful assessment tool in relation to your budget review.

1) **How well does your budget link to your School Development Plan?**

   Are all priorities sufficiently resourced and can this be sustained over the next 3-5 years, if appropriate? Are pupils getting their fair share of the available resources to help them achieve their potential, especially if they are part of under-achieving groups? Are reserves/balances at an appropriate level?

2) **Are staffing levels appropriate to meet the school's needs and are they sustainable within your local and national context?**
Do you use benchmarking to compare teaching and support staff levels with national averages and similar schools? You can refer to the annual school workforce statistics to find out relevant figures at https://www.gov.uk/government/collections/statistics-school-workforce. Do you undertake this review at least annually? Are the results discussed amongst leaders and governors?
Do you question whether your staffing levels are sustainable into the future? Would this be true if funding levels remained the same?
Do you understand how your staffing costs behave when pupil numbers change? At what stage are you unable to absorb increases in rolls and need to employ additional staff (stepped costs)?
What if there was a real terms reduction in funding (i.e. not meeting your individual level of cost pressures) through government driven policy such as the National Funding Formula (NFF)? Are you prepared for any reduction in funding you may be faced with? Can you sustain staffing levels? Would you need to change the mix of teaching and support staff? If you can't keep existing staff, how will this impact on pupil outcomes?

3) **Is paid staff overtime focused, authorised or even necessary?**
Do you have procedures in place to ensure staff overtime is:
   • Agreed in advance by a line manager within the area of work? Is it necessary? What will be the impact with or without this additional work? Should the work have been completed within normal working hours? Who will ensure the work undertaken in this time is quality assured?
   • Authorised in advance by a leader with financial responsibility? Are there sufficient resources allocated in the budget to cover the overtime request? Have the full costs of paid overtime been taken into consideration when allocating resources in the budget, i.e. increased National Insurance contributions, holiday pay and the living wage?

4) **Are there areas of waste/financial inefficiency within the school that need to be addressed?**
How might you identify these? Can they be tackled with no detriment to student outcomes? Over what timescales can savings be made? Have you reviewed all areas of the budget, including those

which may not at first appear to be a relatively high cost, for example consumables such as paper and stationery, printing costs, telephony systems etc.?

5) **Teacher recruitment strategies: are you making the most of the many types of resources available to you?**
Can you be creative to improve your chances of success in teacher recruitment and avoid spiralling staff advertising costs? Are you making the most of low cost media, including social media? Do you have a staff member in school who can manage your use of social media for positive results and in line with safeguarding and e-safety protocols?

6) **Are your supply costs high?**
Is staff absence an issue for you? Do you have a staff wellbeing programme in place to try to reduce absence?
Do your school policies support efficient supply cover management? Examples might include:
- avoiding staff being out of the classroom unless absolutely necessary;
- school trips in holiday time and not always term time;
- support staff supporting trips, particularly in term time, so that fewer teachers require cover;
- fewer staff attending courses but those who do then disseminate information back to colleagues to ensure value for money and efficient sharing of learning and information.

7) **Is your school energy efficient?**
Are your school buildings as energy efficient as possible? Would capital investment help to improve energy efficiency? Are there funding sources available to support this? One example is Salix loans: https://www.salixfinance.co.uk/loans/schools-loans, which are interest-free loans backed by the DfE, repaid from the savings in energy bills achieved through installing energy-efficient technologies.
Do you have an energy efficient culture within school? Do staff and pupils switch lights off when they leave a room and understand the most energy efficient ways to manage IT and electronic equipment? What can you do to create this culture amongst staff and pupils? Are there any links to learning for pupils?
Can your systems support automated shut-down of equipment after a specified time to save energy? Do your IT staff or IT provider understand how to make best use of your systems' functionality to support energy efficiency?

8) **Are buyback arrangements for services and contracts regularly reviewed?**

When buyback arrangements and contracts are up for renewal, is a full value for money review undertaken to ensure the service:

- is still required;
- is appropriately defined in a comprehensive specification;
- meets the needs of the school/learners/other stakeholders;
- is economical (the best deal taking cost and quality into account);
- is managed efficiently with robust monitoring of performance;
- has a positive impact on student outcomes?

Early action is advisable if you are intending to change anything governed by contracts, since it can take considerable time to identify alternative options and arrange tenders if the level of expenditure is above the relevant thresholds.

9) **Are you protected against fraud?**

Does your most recent audit report highlight any areas for concern in relation to fraud prevention? Have you taken action against any areas for concern and followed up all recommendations within the given timescales?

Do you have internal arrangements to undertake interim audit checks in between external audit processes?

Do you undertake a self-assessment as part of the process of completing an annual statement of internal control?

Does your school have robust internal financial procedures and are checks carried out to ensure these are followed by all appropriate staff?

Is there an appropriate segregation of duties amongst staff undertaking finance duties in school?

Is there a culture of transparency, within the limits of confidentiality in some areas, in relation to financial management?

Is your school's whistle blowing policy available for all staff to view on your school website? Do staff know what it is and where to find it?

10) **Do leaders at all levels buy into a culture of efficient and effective resource management and understand the implications of their own day to day decision making?**

Does the school business leader (or equivalent) or senior leader with responsibility for finance regularly brief the rest of the senior leadership team regarding budget updates, future funding scenarios, potential areas of overspending/underspending and the school's financial objectives?

Do senior leaders feel there is shared ownership of the school's financial health, financial leadership and financial success?

Securing a value for money culture

Staff at all levels need to understand what a value for money culture means. There is a common misconception that this means always going for the cheapest option and saving money wherever possible. Terms like 'cuts' and 'savings' tend to feature in many people's description of VfM. But what we really mean by value for money is ensuring that school funding is spent wisely in order to have maximum positive impact on student outcomes. If it doesn't, then why is it needed?

All staff do not need to know and understand every level of the VfM model. They simply need to understand that any spending of school money must impact positively on student outcomes in order for it to be considered good value for money.

So, for example, if £10,000 was proposed to be spent (input) on some curriculum content resources, it would be expected that this resource would enable a significant number of pupils to access many aspects of the curriculum (output). In turn, the fact they had the opportunity to use this resource to aid their learning across the curriculum would contribute to increased pupil outcomes in the way of exam or test results, as well as potentially to the development of their character, citizenship and social action and these outcomes could be measured.

If a smaller amount, say £100, was proposed to be spent (input) on IT equipment it would be expected that this would support learners and/or teachers in the classroom (output). This relatively small amount of equipment may not reach as many pupils as £10,000 worth of curriculum content resource in the example above, in which case the output may be less, but the impact on pupil outcomes may be just as high in terms of its effectiveness.

An even simpler way of communicating the VfM approach to school spending and embedding the culture you want to see in your school is to focus on where resources are being wasted. The principles are exactly the same as in the examples above, but perhaps this is coming at it in a way most people will understand, as we have to manage our own personal finances and we would not expect to pay for our weekly shop and leave with an empty trolley.

Schools can be places where resources are wasted on a regular basis. Some extra time spent analysing your spending patterns in detail should highlight any areas where there may be a significant waste of resources and the time you spend doing this now could save you money in the future.

The hardest part of efficiency exercises such as this is not identifying the area of waste, but rather changing the embedded culture amongst staff to one of value for money awareness, reduced or no waste and spending vigilance. If you can highlight to staff how much money is being wasted in a particular area and how that money could be used more wisely, you may be surprised how quickly you can get staff on board. Avoid apportioning blame for previous spending decisions; remember you are trying to motivate staff to work collaboratively to improve spending patterns, not to feel as though they are being told off.

Review and challenge

The key to success is for schools to regularly review and question their resource allocation to ensure it is as efficient and effective as possible and that it remains that way. A budget review is an ideal exercise to achieve this.

If schools become complacent it is easy for standards to slip. Regular questioning and self-review ensures that you are getting it right or that you know what to change if you are not. Even high performing schools should not be afraid to make changes in the interests of better resource allocation. This will enable you to sustain that high performance.

Governors have a key role to play in ensuring effective resource allocation. They are responsible for ensuring that the school's strategic leadership secures a trend of continuous improvement in all aspects of school life, and specifically in promoting positive pupil outcomes.

Whilst the governor role is not operational, it is important that governors are aware of the school's current financial position and future potential budget scenarios in order to provide adequate challenge and support schools to ensure financial sustainability into the future. This involves more than simply ensuring a school is not in danger of deficit.

Effective governors challenge and support school leaders to allocate resources in the most efficient and effective way to improve pupil outcomes. This is a key part of your value for money culture. We go into more detail about reporting your budget review to governors in Part 4.

The most important question to remember in any resource based decision and at all stages of your budget review is:

"What IMPACT will this have on pupil outcomes?"

This is a particularly useful reflection when you have decisions to make on whether to continue along the same path you are currently following, or make a significant change. The answer to this question may be the justification you need to make changes for the better.

Using benchmarking tools to assess value for money

The main purpose of benchmarking tools is as a means of assessing VfM by triggering thought and discussion into a specific area of the budget by making comparisons with other schools in similar circumstances. The tools should be used to consider pay and non-pay budgets.

Benchmarking will not confirm that your school is right or wrong in the way it allocates resources, but if your spending patterns appear to be considerably different when compared to similar schools, you should ask why and challenge any reasons given until you are satisfied. Your reasons may be justified, even for significant variations, meaning you may decide that no action is required.

Alternatively, the exercise may highlight an area where your spending is significantly higher or lower than other schools in a similar context and this may trigger a full budget review in that area. Ideally, benchmarking results should be shared with others for deeper discussion and context and should be reported to governors annually. The tools can facilitate contact with comparator schools to share their approach in more detail.

You can find more information about value for money among our blog posts at https://schoolfinancialsuccess.com/blogs-2/.

4 SELF-ASSESS PAY BUDGETS

VfM assessment

A fundamental part of your budget review will be a self-assessment of your school's position in relation to pay budgets.

Completing the following checklist for your school, divided between economy, efficiency and effectiveness, will give you an evidence-based assessment of your school's pay budgets, determining how well they represent value for money. You will then be able to establish what action needs to be taken. These actions can be fed directly into your strategic action plan.

Economy:
(getting the best balance of cost and quality)
✓ Are staff paid at an appropriate point on their pay scale or pay range, correctly reflecting their level of responsibility?
✓ Is your appraisal policy and implementation of it rigorous and robust, promoting performance related pay and ensuring there is no upward movement when performance does not warrant it?
✓ Is your school subject to local job evaluation?
✓ If applicable, is job evaluation guidance being correctly followed when setting relevant pay levels?
✓ Do you have a policy for deciding on the level of pay for new posts?
✓ Do you know whether your pay level decisions represent value for money?
Efficiency:
(making the best use of the resources available to you)
✓ Are staff deployed efficiently to get the most output from their working time?

- ✓ Is staff output balanced with quality of provision?
- ✓ Do you have a staff well-being programme to support all staff to perform at their highest level of capability and to reduce levels of staff absence?
- ✓ Do you have knowledge and records of staff qualifications and skills, so that you can ensure all team members are playing to their strengths?
- ✓ Do all staff have access to appropriate and challenging professional development, relevant to their role and level of responsibility?
- ✓ Is external professional development shared amongst colleagues?
- ✓ Are teaching staff deployed to teach for an appropriate number of hours in the timetable cycle, to balance their maximum output with time for Preparation, Planning and Assessment (PPA) and any additional responsibilities they hold (e.g. teaching and learning responsibility (TLR) allowances)?
- ✓ Is there an appropriate spread of task and responsibility amongst support staff that reflects their pay grade?
- ✓ Are support staff used, where appropriate, to cover tasks which support teachers to focus on teaching?
- ✓ Are support staff used, where appropriate, to cover break and lunchtime duties to reduce teacher workload?
- ✓ Are support staff used, where appropriate, to accompany school trips and events, reducing the need for external teaching cover?

Effectiveness:
(maximising the impact on pupil outcomes and school priorities)

- ✓ Are teaching staff appraisal objectives set appropriately in relation to pupil outcomes and school priorities, promoting teacher responsibility for pupils in their care in relation to:
  - • academic progress?
  - • personal development, behaviour and welfare?
  - • SMSC (Social, Moral, Spiritual and Cultural) provision?
- ✓ Do teacher appraisal reviews consist of at least three meetings per year to set objectives, review progress mid-year and assess if targets have been met?
- ✓ Do support staff undertake a process of annual development review to assess and motivate their performance, even if not pay related?
- ✓ Are development review objectives for support staff set in relation to school priorities?
- ✓ Do support staff development reviews consist of at least three meetings per year to set objectives, review progress mid-year and

assess if targets have been met?

✓ Are mechanisms in place for supporting and challenging staff who do not successfully meet their objectives?

✓ Is professional development for all staff recorded and evaluated to assess its impact and inform future decisions on training opportunities for all?

Leadership costs

It is also important to spend some time thinking about the leadership structure in your school, as this represents the most expensive decisions made on staff deployment. This includes middle as well as senior leadership, anyone who holds a TLR allowance, anyone who is paid on the leadership pay range and any support staff members who are part of the leadership team.

Does your leadership structure represent good value for money?

✓ Compare your leadership structure to other similar sized schools with a similar profile of need. What does it tell you? Are there legitimate reasons for any difference?

If your leadership structure is generous, has this built up over many years? Is it an inherited issue?

If your leadership structure is not so generous, are there any issues with capacity that are preventing school priorities from being achieved? Is a lack of capacity in your leadership structure impacting on school performance?

✓ Do the roles and responsibilities within your leadership structure reflect your school's priorities for improvement?

✓ Does the allocation of teaching time to staff within your leadership structure strike an appropriate balance between efficient deployment of staff and adequate time for leadership and management to meet the school's priorities?

✓ Are leaders paid at an appropriate point on their pay scale or pay range, correctly reflecting their level of leadership responsibility?

✓ Have you undertaken a recent review of TLR allowances across the school, ensuring TLRs are necessary, paid at an appropriate level and meeting the school's priorities for improvement?

✓ Have you ensured that the most appropriate staff lead across all school priorities and that responsibilities are not just tagged on to justify posts or salary levels?

✓ Do leaders work collaboratively within and beyond your school to ensure they have maximum impact on pupil outcomes and the school's priorities?

✓ Do leaders generate additional income for the school, perhaps by delivering professional development to others in education, particularly if you are a teaching school?

✓ Do you have a strategy in place for succession planning to prevent an over-reliance on any one individual and a potential gap in skills, should an individual leave?

Even if you identify that your leadership structure requires review, it may not be easy to make changes as quickly as you would like. You should have plans in place for your ideal structure so that you can move towards this in stages, should there be any opportunity arising from staff turnover.

Be careful to make a regular judgement about your input into this area against your expected savings. It may take a considerable amount of leadership time to undertake a full review of pay budgets. Have you allocated the most appropriate leaders with available time and expertise to do this? If you have chosen to buy in any external advice or support in this area, do the expected benefits and savings outweigh the costs?

5 IDENTIFY NON-PAY AREAS FOR REVIEW

Your school context

With so many non-pay budget areas you may find it is not appropriate or feasible to review all of them. This chapter supports you to identify the key areas for review which will have the biggest overall impact.

Although they may represent only a relatively small proportion of your overall budget, non-pay areas can provide significant potential for positive change in a budget review. There are bound to be areas of complexity, but also opportunities for improving efficiency and reducing waste, especially if this is the first time a budget review has been undertaken.

Every school is different and you need to make your budget review work for you, in your context. Start by thinking about what is important to your school and why.

For example:

- are you facing falling rolls and need to raise your profile in the local community, putting pressure on marketing and events budgets?
- is your building old and in need of repair or refurbishment, causing additional pressure on site related budgets?
- do you have a building that is new and full of sophisticated equipment, putting pressure on equipment maintenance budgets?
- is your IT equipment and/or infrastructure badly in need of updating and a refresh?
- do you need to support transport costs, uniform costs or provision of resources for your pupils?

Establish the issues that are specific to your school and keep them in mind throughout the process.

Areas of focus

It is important to ensure you have selected the most appropriate areas of focus in your budget review, without ignoring any key areas. Be careful not to create protected budgets, whether intentionally or unintentionally. Everyone should be expected to find more efficient ways of doing things and nothing should be sacrosanct. You can encourage managers to come up with their own ideas, which you can then review to decide whether they are appropriate.

Whilst no budget area should be ignored during a full budget review, it is sensible to pay attention to areas of high spending, where effecting change will make a significant monetary saving. It is also important to ensure that the effort you are putting into each area of your review, whether it be time spent or the buying in of external expertise, is proportionate to the likely savings benefit in those areas.

A key strategy throughout the budget review is to identify the barriers that are preventing you from adjusting spending in a particular area and then consider whether you can remove them. For example, is it staff resistance to change which is making introducing a new and potentially more cost-effective way of working difficult? How can you motivate staff to be on board with the proposed change? We discuss this further in chapter 11.

Remember, a budget review isn't solely about saving money. The focus is of course on reducing waste and promoting a VfM culture, but as well as making savings this also means ensuring adequate funding is available to make the school's priorities happen. You need to make sure that any reductions don't have an unacceptably adverse impact on priorities including achievement, teaching and learning, behaviour and attendance.

It is therefore also useful to consider budget areas where you expect change will have the least detrimental impact to your school's priorities. Any background changes that would achieve savings and would not be noticed by staff and pupils are a good place to start. Examples might include a review of your telephony system and set-up, review of support contracts, or a review of your banking arrangements to ensure you are making the most of savings available from using direct debit facilities.

This doesn't mean you should be afraid to consider areas where change could have a detrimental impact on pupil outcomes and other school priorities. You may decide not to implement any change, but due consideration is necessary to ensure a thorough and rigorous process. Ideas could be triggered that would otherwise not have been thought of.

For example, you may be concerned about reviewing printing and photocopying budgets in case restrictions are contentious to staff and pupils, make life harder or impact negatively on pupil outcomes. If you feel there is potential waste in this budget area, you should still identify it for review and make sure all angles are considered when recommendations are being drawn up.

Try to ensure that your recommendations are a balance of financial and practical common sense, which can be bought into by all stakeholders as part of the change management process.

Honest and accurate self-assessment

You and the other leaders in your school know your school well, so it is important to be honest in your reflections and listen to your instinct. Do you know there are areas of the budget which do not represent value for money? Have you been avoiding implementing change because it is difficult, hard work or time-consuming?

If you are serious about undertaking a successful budget review, now is the time to go for it, regardless of how big the challenge may seem. Keep reminding yourself of your over-arching objectives and your motivation for embarking on the review in the first place.

For any budget areas you choose to review you should:
- assess the risks to pupil outcomes and other school priorities;
- be prepared to come up with alternative creative and innovative ways of working;
- consider the extent of the change - is there a middle ground that achieves some savings without a complete overhaul and the risk of negative consequences?

Some examples of budget areas where review may achieve change, reduce waste and initiate savings are shown below. Services and contracts will vary from school to school, depending on your set-up and a range of other factors.

Services could include:
- Cleaning arrangements
- Catering arrangements
- Sanitary disposal
- Refuse removal
- Grounds maintenance
- Building Management services
- Equipment Maintenance Agreements
- IT services
- Data Management services

- Payroll services
- HR Admin and Advisory services
- Legal Services

Support contracts could include:
- IT infrastructure, i.e. servers, broadband, wireless connectivity etc.
- IT learning software
- IT systems software
- IT hardware
- Building Management hardware and software
- Security Systems/Access control hardware and software
- CCTV hardware and software
- Reprographics machines and printers
- Lift Maintenance Support

Other budget areas for review include:
- Use of agency cover staff
- Telephony
- Printing and Photocopying
- Hire of Transport/Vehicle Running Costs
- Postage
- IT Equipment/Consumables

6 MAXIMISE INCOME OPPORTUNITIES

Your school context

Many schools have existing areas of income generation within their budget plan. This will look different for each school; for some schools there may be none at all. In a future publication, we will be exploring ideas and offering advice for developing an income generation strategy, as a strategic working plan which can be continually developed over time to support a school's long-term financial sustainability.

This chapter focuses on how you can ensure that the existing income streams planned in your budget are providing the best opportunities for income generation to support your budget review.

Regardless of the relative size of your income streams, you will achieve good value for money and promote proper compliance and best practice if you ensure that your procedures for managing income are robust. Sound income controls will protect against waste and fraud, maximising the opportunities available to you.

Start by thinking about what opportunities for income generation are already being implemented by your school.

For example:

- Do you hire school facilities to the local community, local businesses, other schools or other organisations outside of the school day?
- Do you sell any items such as pupil resources to parents and carers?
- Do you sell items of equipment that you no longer use to other stakeholders?
- Are your pupils or other stakeholder groups involved in fund-raising activities?
- Do you receive cash back incentives for any of your areas of procurement?
- Do you bid for external grants?

Examples of categories of income

1) Applications for external funding

Making applications for external funding or bid writing is a well-known way for schools to secure funding for project-based initiatives with a specific objective. The bid submission would usually include a business plan. If successful, the school would need to monitor and evaluate the use of the funding, often reporting back to the funding organisation to ensure accountability for its use.

2) School-to-school support

Originally the remit of teaching schools, all schools are becoming more aware and proactive when it comes to charging for school-to-school support where appropriate. If a school has staff expertise, intellectual capital, training capacity and resources that are sought after by other schools or educational organisations, this can be a valid source of additional income.

3) Sharing staff and services

There are many examples of schools working creatively to make efficiency savings, in particular staff working collaboratively to share services such as site, finance and human resource teams. This is inevitably more commonplace across multi-academy trusts but can also be seen among schools who collaborate less formally.

Where this approach generates additional income for a school is when staff with specialist expertise are provided to schools which need that support but can't afford a full-time member of staff with those skills.

Schools who have capacity and appropriate equipment have been known to offer printing and design services to local businesses and other schools in the area.

4) Making the most of premises

Some schools hire out their premises outside of the school day to community groups, individuals and local businesses. This could include the hire of the facility and other extras such as car parking, use of IT equipment and catering for meetings and events. Offering timetabled events such as adult education classes and fitness classes outside of school hours is also popular among schools.

Some schools have brought catering in-house to provide more flexibility so that they can then offer catering as part of a more attractive lettings package. This can be further developed into on-site cafés which generate income from pupils, staff and visitors.

Even if indoor spaces aren't sought after for hire, schools are being creative with the hire of outdoor facilities too, with examples of schools teaming up with a car boot sale organiser who pays the school a percentage from each car's entry fee. Car parks can be offered as additional parking facilities for nearby events at a cost to the event's organisers.

If premises are in abundance, it is possible to enter into lettings arrangements and service level agreements which generate full-time income, in accommodation that is not used by the school for its core purpose.

5) Selling items to/charging parents

Selling items to parents is becoming increasingly popular in schools, with some citing the following as examples which generate a percentage of income for the school:

- Annual school photos
- One-off promotions, such as hooded jumpers with pupil names on the back at the end of the school year, or school year books

Other examples of sales to parents include learning resources which enhance curriculum delivery, such as:

- Textbooks
- Software licences
- IT equipment

6) Securing passive income

Some schools have taken the opportunity to set up revenue streams which continue to bring in money without significant further effort. An example of this is income generated from solar panels or other energy initiatives such as wind turbines. You must check first with the owner of the land and buildings that you have the right to make such changes, and take legal advice on the contracts to avoid any risks.

Often these examples require some capital investment, but for schools who embark on such initiatives at the right time, capital funding may be available to cover these costs. If not, a business plan will need to show the payback period, i.e. the length of time it will take for the school's own capital investment to be paid back and pure 'profit' to start to be generated. This is clearly a different type of income generation to that of traditional fund-raising activities for a specific purpose.

7) Fund-raising

Fund-raising is commonplace in schools and has the bonus of teaching young people about the importance of charity, making a positive contribution to the world and being part of something bigger than themselves. In these instances, this would not represent income generation for schools. However, traditionally school related groups such as a Parent Teacher Association (PTA) may generate funds to pay for big one-off school items such as a school mini-bus. In the current financial climate, some schools may choose to raise funds for their own purposes or seek sponsorship and support from other local organisations and businesses.

Reviewing income controls

Charging and Remissions Policy

The DfE offers advice to local authority maintained schools on charging for school activities at:

https://www.gov.uk/government/publications/charging-for-school-activities.

It will help to ensure your charging policy is adequate and that you are aware of the various situations that could arise for schools when charging stakeholders, particularly parents.

Under the charging provisions set out in legislation, a charging policy is essential for any school that chooses to charge for defined activities. The policy must be made available to parents on request. Academies (including free schools, studio schools and university technical colleges) are required to comply with the law on charging for school activities, through their funding agreements. This guidance is therefore an invaluable reference document if you are in an academy.

School governing bodies and local authorities **cannot** charge for:
- an admission application to any state-funded school;
- education provided during school hours (including the supply of any materials, books, instruments or other equipment);
- education provided outside school hours if it is part of the national curriculum or part of a syllabus for a prescribed public examination that the pupil is being prepared for at the school, or part of religious education;
- instrumental or vocal tuition, for pupils learning individually or in groups, unless the tuition is provided at the request of the pupil's parent;

- entry for a prescribed public examination, if the pupil has been prepared for it at the school; and
- examination re-sit(s) if the pupil is being prepared for the re-sit(s) at the school.

School governing bodies and local authorities **can** charge for:
- any materials, books, instruments, or equipment, where the child's parent wishes him/her to own them;
- optional extras;
- music and vocal tuition, in limited circumstances;
- certain early years provision;
- community facilities.

Schools must ensure that they inform parents on low incomes and in receipt of certain benefits about the support available to them if they are being asked for contributions towards the cost of school visits.

The guidance from the DfE focuses mainly on charging parents. However, as we have seen from the examples of types of income, there are other stakeholder groups whom you might need to charge.

The groups you expect to charge, and the activities or services for which you intend to charge them, should be clearly explained in your charging policy. You should also explain the method of payment that will be available to each group. For example, will you accept cash, will you raise an invoice or do you have any other methods? You should include clear information giving the rationale for calculating charges to different groups for different types of activity.

Ethical practice

If your school is involved in fund-raising activities to support income generation, it is important that ethical practice is followed at all times and in all circumstances. Certain activities, such as bag packing in local supermarkets, require a registered charity number. Fund-raising under such a registration must only be done for the benefit of the associated charity. Always be clear what you are raising money for and make sure there is a clear audit trail of evidence to prove that any monies raised were used for the prescribed purpose.

Debt management

Audit trail and process are extremely important in income management to ensure that the income raised is collected or received and is then dealt with correctly. Wherever possible, money should be collected before the activity takes place. If this is not practicable, a written commitment to pay should be obtained before any associated costs are paid out. If the anticipated income is not received it becomes a bad debt, which can cause an overspend if you have budgeted for it.

Debt management systems should be in place to keep a track of any monies owed to the school and payments should be chased on a timely basis according to financial procedures. Recovery of bad debts should increase in intensity as the debt grows older and if the debt remains unpaid, the debtor should not be allowed to partake in any activity with the school until such a time as the debt is cleared. Even then, it is at your discretion as to whether or not you would choose to provide a service repeatedly to someone with a poor payment history.

Ensure you have the full details of the customer or potential debtor as part of your agreement to provide any service or activity, including a variety of contact details such as telephone number, email and physical address. This will give you alternative methods of communication should you be unsuccessful in chasing payment using one method.

If you buy into a debt management service from your LA or any other provider, make sure you understand how their systems work. Know what the stages of debt recovery are and what your school's responsibilities are. You may think your income has been received if it has been posted to your accounts, but if at the end of the year the debt remains outstanding, your income account could be debited to cancel out the bad debt, which has the same effect as an overspend in your accounts if you have budgeted for it.

Internal and external audit

It is wise to keep a regular check on any systems you have in place to make sure they continue to be fit for purpose. Your internal and/or external audit assessment will give you some reassurance (or otherwise) of your overall compliance, but audit is also very useful and effective as an internal school management tool. Hopefully you will not uncover any major flaws in your systems once you have your financial procedures in place, but even the most confident and successfully financially managed schools can make alterations and improvements to increase the robustness of systems and controls.

Financial procedures for income

Ultimately, all of the systems you have in place will be recorded in your school's own internal financial procedures, which are discussed in the next chapter.

In relation to income, you would expect to see roles and responsibilities clearly described for the different stages of the income management process. There must be a segregation of duties so that more than one person is involved in the income process from beginning to end. This significantly reduces the risk of fraud and acts as a layered check to ensure that procedures are followed correctly and income is properly recorded.

Banking procedures should also be detailed here, with particular reference to the process of how income gets into the bank in a timely manner. It is not good practice for cash or cheques to be left on the school premises for prolonged periods of time. For the short time in between banking deposits, ideally no more than one week, money should be stored safely and securely in a secure and fire-proof safe with limited access by authorised personnel only. Even the banking process itself can carry great risk. Many schools now use a cash collection service to reduce the risk to staff in transporting large amounts of money.

How income is posted into the chart of accounts is another important consideration. Do all staff in the team know and understand how this works and know which codes to use? Your internal audit checks should highlight if processes are not being followed correctly, so that specific training can be given where necessary.

Financial procedures cover all areas of financial management and are the cornerstone of sound financial management in schools and strong internal controls. We will therefore now move on from income to look at financial procedures in the widest sense.

7 REVIEW FINANCIAL PROCEDURES

Context

All schools, regardless of their status, must adhere to financial procedures which are externally driven, i.e. the Scheme for Financing Schools for LA schools, and the Academies Financial Handbook. These procedures outline what schools can expect from funding bodies and what funding bodies can expect from schools in the way of financial management. They provide a clear delineation of responsibilities and there can be serious consequences if a school does not follow them.

Individual schools must also have their own internal financial procedures, which should detail all the financial management processes undertaken by the school. This is an important requirement, as processes and procedures will differ from school to school. Having bespoke procedures will ensure overall compliance with the external frameworks described above.

Schools use different finance systems, have varying finance team structures, and buy in differing levels of support from the LA or other professional organisations. All of these things impact on what a school's detailed processes might look like. For example, segregation of duties will be approached differently in a school with a finance team of five staff compared with a smaller school which may only have one person working on finance.

These procedures will detail levels of authorisation within the school team across all the different areas of financial management such as payroll, banking arrangements and procurement. They should be truly bespoke to the individual school and offer a high level of detail and clarity to any stakeholder who may have an interest, especially governors and auditors.

Internal financial procedures should be reviewed and updated on an annual basis, usually ready for governor approval at the beginning of the new academic year. It is wise, however, to complete a critical review as part of your budget review exercise.

You may find that savings can be made simply by tightening up procedures in some areas. These are the type of background savings which probably won't have a detrimental impact on school priorities, as they are unlikely to be noticed by staff and pupils.

There is potential for savings to be made across both pay and non-pay budgets through a review of procedures. One example is reducing staff time spent in correcting errors or chasing up issues. There is also scope to make monetary savings. Do you have appropriate spending levels in place for key staff, so that other staff who hold them to account can ask challenging questions during the checking and authorisation process? This will avoid transactions being processed without due care and attention.

Do you have a cap on how much staff can claim back through petty cash, to avoid poorly controlled spending from capitation budgets? Is your frequency and detail of reporting to budget holders sufficient to enable them to manage their budgets effectively? Without adequate controls in place, each of these areas, and more, can quickly become lax and lead to overspending.

VfM checklist

Use the following checklist to ensure your financial procedures are working to promote your value for money culture:

✓ Do you have adequate payroll checking procedures in place to ensure that staff are not overpaid, even by a relatively small amount?

✓ Do you have robust and rigorous checking of direct charges to your bank account e.g. by the LA or from the use of an online purchasing card?

✓ Are procedures in place to ensure best value checks are undertaken for each potential order before commitments are made on the finance system? While the formal framework of best value is no longer a requirement, the principles remain worth pursuing.

✓ Do all staff involved in financial processing understand these procedures, the reasons for them (why), how to achieve best value (how) and what tasks and checks need to be carried out (what)? Is training needed?

✓ Do all staff, particularly those who make requests for funds to be spent, also understand these procedures and know what part they play in achieving best value?

✓ Do the procedures detail sufficient layers of authorisation and segregation of duties in the procurement process?

✓ Do you have strong controls in place for income management to avoid bad debts, properly record all income in a timely manner and prevent fraud?

8 COLLABORATION AND PARTNERSHIPS

Overview

While many schools share ideas and learning strategies on a regular basis, it is sometimes thought that financial collaboration can only occur if schools are working together in formal or informal partnerships such as MATs or soft and hard federations.

These arrangements are indeed a means to access joint purchasing, as an example, but they are not the only way for schools to work together to make savings. If schools can work collaboratively for financial efficiency, then there are more resources available to deliver a high-quality education provision for all. It seems obvious.

However, the biggest challenge to this way of thinking for schools is local competition. Schools are funded based on pupil numbers and in many cases local competition to secure admissions is fierce. Why then would one school want to help another school to be better? The answer is simple. Because our children deserve it!

In reality the picture is not so simple. Ideas for financial collaboration such as sharing staff may have a higher success rate if the schools are closely positioned geographically. This however, introduces the element of local competition. Where schools can accept this and find a mutually agreeable arrangement, the quality of provision to all pupils in those schools can be improved.

Procurement

Collaborating in procurement is an area that is more likely to be successful even when competition is a factor. All schools naturally want to keep costs down and share the workload. What you then do with the service and how it works in your own school can be personalised to each individual school involved.

The two main areas of benefit are achieving discounts for bulk orders and sharing the administrative costs of procurement. For an already established MAT or other Trust, this is possibly one of the advantages of working together that was achieved when the trust was first set up. You should make sure you regularly review your arrangements as a trust, or group of schools, to ensure you are still getting value for money for all the schools involved. This should be a key part of your budget review if you are a school that is part of a MAT or other Trust.

If your school is not part of a MAT or other collaborative set-up, one way of achieving economies of scale is to use the local authority. As with any provider, you need to establish that their contracts are comprehensive enough and that they achieve good value. By this we mean an appropriate balance between price and quality.

An alternative solution is to join forces with other schools in the same position as you, and work together informally to reap the benefits that can come from collaboration.

As a school procuring goods and services alone, you are likely to pay the full price. If you can work with other schools, discounts will usually be available for high volume transactions. The supplier makes savings because they only have to deal with one central person for the order, invoicing and payment aspects of the transaction, and they are shifting goods or services faster. It doesn't prevent schools from splitting up the order for delivery to different sites.

What collaborative procurement does require is one school willing to take the lead, collating the requirements from individual schools and dealing with the supplier on their behalf. This arrangement is usual in a MAT or other type of trust and can easily be set up for schools who are working together informally. A service level agreement between the schools is an efficient way of protecting the lead school from any risks in taking on this responsibility. It would be entirely reasonable for the lead school to make a small charge to the other schools for this service; this can be done by applying a percentage overhead to the price paid for the goods or services. You may want to consider acting as the lead school to achieve financial savings in informal collaboration with other schools if it supports the success of your budget review, helps you to meet your over-arching objectives and if you have the capacity to do so.

One of the challenges that schools face with collaborative procurement is agreeing a specification for a product or service. In some cases, this may be straightforward, and in others each school may have different requirements. It may be possible to procure a flexible solution which meets the differing needs of all the schools in the group and still saves money. Otherwise, some level of compromise may be needed. It would fall upon the lead school to either negotiate the flexible solution or facilitate a compromise between schools if appropriate.

It is vital that the person taking charge on behalf of the schools has a sound knowledge of the product or service being procured and can use that specialist knowledge in the negotiation process. The capacity and expertise of school staff may determine which school will take the lead in each individual procurement exercise.

There are also other vehicles for collaborative procurement, such as regional arrangements. The DfE School Financial Health and Efficiency web pages contain information about effective procurement and examples of collaboration:

https://www.gov.uk/government/collections/schools-financial-health-and-efficiency.

This information is worth checking out, especially if there aren't any obvious opportunities using your existing contacts in the local area.

DfE has also published a buying strategy for schools, which contains practical guidance and links to specific resources, including details of initiatives the Department is introducing, such as buying hubs and National Deals for specific items. It can be found at:

https://www.gov.uk/government/publications/schools-buying-strategy.

9 SUMMARY CHECKLIST: BUDGET REVIEW LEADER ROLE

A recap

Before you initiate any involvement from the teams you have formed for your budget review, let's recap what you should have in place so far and what you need to communicate to your teams:

The budget review leader should have:
- ✓ undertaken pre-work to understand:
  - the concept of value for money
  - the school budget and links to the school development plan
- ✓ reviewed financial procedures and implemented changes
- ✓ prepared a budget review strategic action plan which includes:

  Introduction:
  - over-arching objectives and success criteria
  - reporting of outcomes
  - overall timeline

  Pay budgets:
  - self-assessment of your school's position in relation to pay budgets
  - actions
  - timeline
  - resources
  - implementation and monitoring

  Non-pay budgets:
  - identification of non-pay budget areas for review
  - objectives and success criteria for individual budget areas
  - formation of teams for each area of review
  - timelines for review completion for each area

- implementation and monitoring

Income budgets (if applicable):

- identification of existing income opportunities
- review of income controls
- actions
- timeline
- resources
- implementation and monitoring

✓ considered opportunities for collaboration, feeding them into the strategic action plan

✓ communicated the plan so far to teams highlighting the following:

- overall objective for relevant budget areas within the review
- timeline for completion
- available resources to conduct the review and the process for requesting additional resource if appropriate
- mechanisms for assessing progress and reporting outcomes to the budget review leader
- to whom the outcomes of the whole budget review will be reported.

Part 2: Remit of Teams

10 REVIEW APPROACH

Team focus

In a secondary school or a large primary school, you are likely to have a team of staff working on a particular budget review area, in order to break the task up and make it more manageable. It is the remit of the team in each budget area to develop the relevant parts of the strategic action plan according to their own investigations and expertise in that area. If you have followed our advice so far, they should already understand why they are being asked to look at a specific area of the budget review and the objective they are trying to meet, following the budget review leader's communications to them. What they will do and how they will achieve that objective is their key focus.

Each team should co-ordinate the review for their budget area and regularly provide feedback to the budget review leader, who will ensure there are no overlaps or duplication of work and that all areas are being covered adequately with no gaps.

Of course, not all schools are big enough to warrant several different teams working on a budget review. In smaller schools, there may be very few staff involved, or the review may even be undertaken by only one person. This process is still useful as a step-by-step guide of how to approach the task. It is, for example, still important to outline the overall budget review strategic action plan before getting into the detailed work in each specific budget area. This ensures you have a coherent and consistent approach throughout your budget review and that you stay focused on the overall task in hand.

A strategic action plan may also help the person to whom you are accountable to understand the scope and scale of the review that you are undertaking. This is essential if you find yourself being pulled in all directions and need to ask for help, or get agreement on which other priorities can be allowed to slip.

In the third part of this book we give some examples of the sorts of issues and solutions that teams or individuals taking on a review may deal with in the process of their review. These can differ quite significantly from one budget area to another.

Key areas of change

There are three key areas of change that budget review teams will need to address. These are:

- leading cultural change
- managing system procedural change
- developing an operational action plan for a specific budget review area.

As we have already seen, some areas of the budget review may involve background changes to operations and procedures which have little visible effect for the majority of stakeholders. These are often easier areas to tackle and can usually be done relatively quickly. An example might be reviewing telephony set-up, the number of line rentals and mechanisms for paying bills.

The more technical or complex the issue, the more time it will take, but the need for leading cultural change is usually not as evident in these scenarios.

When areas of the budget review are in the foreground of school life and impact on the visible operations of the school and the behaviours of stakeholders, in particular staff and pupils, then leading cultural change is critical. An example of this type of change is the school's printing and photocopying arrangements, where changes to systems and procedures could impact on many staff and pupils and could be perceived to make their lives more difficult. It will be your judgement call as to whether the potential benefit from making the change justifies the effort involved.

11 LEADING CULTURAL CHANGE

Theory of change

"Change is the only constant."
Heraclitus, Greek philosopher

When you become focused on improving financial efficiency, it is very easy to get deeply embroiled in processes and the potential for saving money, sometimes disregarding the true cost of the potential change. If you want the change you are proposing to be effective and sustainable, you need to identify the people who are affected by the change and consider what their reaction is likely to be.

Having been through a long and in-depth process of analysis and review, you are in the privileged position of having all the information, understanding the need for change and being able to envisage a different way which is more cost effective. This means you are ahead of your colleagues in appreciating what it may mean; they need time and information to enable them to catch up.

Have you considered what the impact will be on staff, pupils and other stakeholders? You need to! A change which is reliant on people's behaviours will only be effective and sustainable if everyone in the school believes in it and buys into it.

To secure people's buy-in it can be very useful to show **why** the change is needed, **how** you plan to achieve the change and **what** you expect from them as an individual or team. We will refer to this as the **why, how, what** approach. Let's consider each step in more detail.

1) **Why** is the change needed?

Ask yourself why is this change even necessary? What's wrong with things as they are now? If people understand the reasons behind the need for change, they are more likely to buy into it.

The best way to sell the 'why' of your change is to focus on the benefits. What's in it for the individual? What's in it for the organisation? It is very useful to put this into a context that means something to the audience you are selling the change to. In the case of financial savings for a school, you may share some of the background as to why your budget review is needed, but unless they are working at a senior level and can really understand these reasons and their implications, then you will probably lose them if you labour it too much, so be brief, hard-hitting and to the point.

The trick is then to contextualise the benefits into something that is meaningful to them, either as an individual in your school or for the team they belong to and are invested in. Try to give an example, such as the funding released from one budget area through financial savings being equivalent to the cost of an extra member of staff or the cost of some new technology in school that would make their lives easier.

Be sure not to make promises that you do not intend to keep. If you are making a comparison to help people to see the value of a saving, be clear that it is only for illustrative purposes. You don't want a disappointed group of staff when the savings that they contribute to making are re-directed to an entirely different initiative from the one they were hoping for. Trust, honesty and integrity are critical leadership characteristics for effective change management.

2) **How** do you plan to bring about change?

Next you need to share with people 'how' the change will be brought about. Is there a system or process that will be followed to achieve the change?

It is essential to convey how you plan to make the change in order for the people involved to know it is achievable. What process will be followed? How long will it take? How will you know if it has been a success? The level of detail you give at this point is dependent on your audience in terms of size and the level they are working at.

If you are working with a relatively small team who are all heavily invested in the change, they may appreciate more detail and a deeper understanding of the process. This may be necessary if their contribution to the review is substantial.

If you are presenting to a large staff body, you need to ensure the level of detail is relative to 'what' you will be asking them to do (which we explain in the next section). They won't want to hear a detailed run-down of the technical process behind an organisation-wide reprographics review if all you want them to do is select a different code on the photocopier. Make it relevant and to the point and you will be more likely to hold their attention.

3) **What** do you expect from the individual or team?

If you have been convincing in describing the 'why' and the 'how', people will be eager to know 'what' you expect from them as an individual or as a team. What behaviours do you want them to demonstrate, in facilitating the successful change? This is an opportunity to show them how they can contribute to the shared success and how valuable their role is in achieving the objective.

Explain exactly what it is you want them to do. Be clear and be specific. Emphasise the importance of their contribution and the team effort (if you are addressing more than one person) that is needed to bring about the change.

Explaining and describing the behaviour you want to see is an important starting point, but continually modelling that behaviour is what will embed the change for the long-term.

Consider getting a smaller team of staff on board first, who you know will have a positive view of the change. If you, and they, are consistently modelling the behaviour you want to see, this will help to convince and encourage others to do the same.

Let's use the '**why, how, what**' approach to consider **why** leadership and management of cultural change is so important, **how** it can be achieved using formal change models and **what** communication is necessary for the people involved.

Why lead and manage change?

People are creatures of habit. It's a common phrase and it's noticeable in everyday life in every context. Think about your school. Do people tend to sit in the same place or close to the same people in 'regular' meetings, staff briefings, and their social time? Do people follow the same daily routine in the organisation of their day?

Even the most forward-thinking, outward-looking, flexible, adaptable and responsive change managers find a comfort in routine and habit in some areas of their lives. It is human nature. It is the reason why, if we are lucky enough to bring our own children into the world, we hear the repeated chants of 'routine', 'routine', 'routine' from our loved ones who are looking out for us. Across generations of human evolution, we crave some security and comfort from routine in our lives.

Staff in schools are busy and are challenged in their roles on a daily basis. No two days are the same in a school. We are all expected to be quick-thinking, responsive and able to carry out firefighting as well as being visionary, strategic and adaptable. So it is understandable that sometimes people would like some things to just stay the same. There is so much fast-paced change in every other area of our working lives that it would be nice for something mundane and operational like photocopying or signing in not to become the biggest challenge and most complex task of the day.

A change you might see as being relatively minor, in comparison to the sometimes alarming levels of waste and overspending you may have uncovered, may be anything but minor to someone else.

But if as a team, or an individual, you have identified a need for change, then it is your job to convince others that this change is a good thing and get them on board with it.

What's in it for me?

The benefits to you, as the change leader, are plentiful.

As a leader, you care about your organisation and its success. If change is led proactively and effectively, minimising opposition, then the new way of working can be implemented quickly and smoothly and the benefits to the school and its stakeholders can be felt sooner.

You are also likely to be ambitious and it is possible that you are actively pursuing career progression or are at least mindful of your career prospects. Leadership of significant change that brings about substantial positive impact can improve your potential for professional opportunities in the future, building a proven track record and developing the credibility that all employers are looking for.

Importantly, there is also a sense of achievement and satisfaction to be gained from leading such major change, knowing that you are making a difference to the lives of young people and their future chances of success. You are also likely to be making a positive difference to your colleagues.

Whatever your drive and motivation, leadership of change can be a highly rewarding experience.

How to manage change using formal leadership models

There are several different approaches to change management that organisations take. There is no evidence to prove that one technique is more or less effective than another and many have something valuable to offer. The trick is to find an approach that suits the context of your organisation, the circumstances you are in at this time and the need for change.

Change leadership models can be useful during your process as a reference point to support teams to implement change smoothly and effectively. They create options for dealing with those difficult circumstances which you will inevitably encounter when you lead any change.

Effective change leaders commonly display attributes of self-awareness, self-management, social awareness and relationship management. They are sensitive and inspiring to others, and can deal with day to day problems without getting distracted from the change they are introducing. The best change leaders use change management models with care, to help them to interpret a situation or challenge.

Whichever model you decide suits you, your organisation and your situation best, it is likely to be used in the background by teams as a set of guidelines to assist the front-facing work that is being undertaken with staff and other stakeholders.

The common theme that runs throughout most change management models is communication, where skills and strategies are critical for any change management process to be successful.

Leadership Models

There are five leadership models which we feel can be useful to support the leadership of change within an organisation.

Leadership that Gets Results	Daniel Goleman	Goleman popularised the idea of emotional intelligence and identified six key leadership styles: Affiliative Authoritative Coaching Democratic Pace-setting Coercive He imagines these styles as a set of golf clubs, with the best players knowing instinctively when to use each club at the right time to get the best results. See Appendix 2 for a further explanation of each style and when it is most effective.
Situational Leadership	Paul Hershey	Categorises all leadership styles into four behavioural types:

	and Ken Blanchard	Directing Coaching Supporting Delegating Designed to give choices for dealing with different situations and to identify personal preferences.

Framework for Leadership	Michael Fullan	Consists of three personality characteristics: energy, enthusiasm and hope, plus five core components of leadership:
		    Moral purpose
		    Understanding change
		    Relationship building
		    Knowledge creation and sharing
		    Coherence making
		Fullan argues that real change is messy and the presence of the five themes plus commitment results in more success.

Agreement and Certainty Matrix	Ralph Stacey	Ralph Stacey argues that many leadership models are characterised by stability and predictability. In contrast, his model assumes a fast-paced world where different skill sets and alternative processes are needed, with a higher level of interaction needed to deal with complexities.
Transformational Leadership	Beverly Alimo-Metcalfe	Transformational leadership is about visionary leadership that has a positive unifying effect on people. This concept is expanded upon in our presentation below of Kotter's eight-step process for leading change.

Kotter's eight-step process for leading change is an extension of the transformational leadership concept and provides a useful and clear summary which might help you lead change during a budget review.

Create urgency	• Spark motivation, get things moving. • Discuss the risks of not making the change. What will it mean for the financial position of your school? • Discuss the opportunities that the change will bring if successful. Will you be able to redirect resources for greater impact? • Give people the chance to ask questions and get involved. Do others have suggestions for your budget review that you haven't thought of? Kotter believed that an organisation needed 75% buy-in for a change to be successful. Spend time and work hard to get this step right before moving on to the next steps.
Form a powerful coalition	• Form a group who you know will show support for the change. For your budget review, this could be your senior leader colleagues. • Ideally, you will enlist a mix of stakeholders to champion the change. Governors are another key group to get on board in a budget review.
Create a vision for change	• Explain the values that are central to your change process. For your budget review, this is more than the reasons that have triggered the review in the first place; it is about the type of organisation you want to be and how a value for money culture is integral to that. • Share an inspirational picture of a future that people will want to be part of. Imagine taking people on a journey in their minds where more can be done with less because there is more focus, less waste and greater impact which reflects positively on everyone in the school community.
Communicate the vision	• Talk about your vision frequently and purposefully at every opportunity. For your

	budget review, this goes beyond opportunities in formal meetings. You can be spreading the key messages as you go about your daily role in school. • Walk the talk and demonstrate the behaviours you want to see in others. Your integrity as a leader is critical here. Practice what you preach and show others there are more innovative and cost-effective ways of working whenever possible.
Remove obstacles	• If there are any processes or structures that are holding up change, you need to focus your attention here. For example, there may still be some individuals within your school who are not on board with the changes being suggested in the budget review. How can you convince them? Spend time working on this and be sure to recognise and reward the people who do make things happen and display the behaviours you are asking for.
Create short-term wins	• Look for low-risk, low-cost, easy to achieve projects. • Thoroughly analyse the pros and cons of your proposed quick wins. If you don't succeed here, it could put the success of your budget review at risk.
Build on the change	• Real change runs deep. Quick wins are only the beginning of what needs to be done to achieve long-term change. What you can do: • After every quick win, analyse what went right, and what needs improving. • Set goals to continue building on the momentum you've achieved. • Keep ideas fresh by bringing in new change agents and leaders for your change coalition.
Embed the change within your culture	What you can do: • Talk about progress every chance you get. Tell success stories about the budget review and encourage others to keep talking about it and the principles behind it.

	• Talk about the school's value for money culture when hiring and training new staff. • Continue to recognise and reward the behaviours you want to see that demonstrate the VfM culture. • Create succession plans to replace key leaders who have contributed to the budget review as they move on, encouraging other staff to get involved in the process of continuous improvement.

What to communicate to support change leadership

Communication is the single most important aspect of any change management process. From research and analysis stage to implementation, your budget review demands effective communication across all stakeholder groups. This is best kept simple and succinct. Initially, the budget review leader needs to communicate effectively to the budget review teams. This then widens to all staff, and later to other stakeholders, particularly pupils when appropriate.

Communicating effectively

Effective communication can often be defined as 'shared meaning', requiring four components that are working together perfectly:

- The individual sending the message must present the message **clearly** and in detail, and radiate **integrity and authenticity**.
- The person receiving the message must decide to **listen**, ask questions for **clarity**, and **trust** the sender of the message.
- The **delivery method** chosen must suit the circumstances and the needs of both the sender and the receiver.
- The **content** of the message has to resonate and **connect**, on some level, with the **already-held beliefs** of the receiver. It must contain the information that the listener wants to hear. It must answer their most cherished and cared about questions.

Effective communication is one of the most difficult issues in any organisation but its importance must not be underestimated, particularly when it comes to organisational change. You cannot over-communicate but even so, it is unlikely that everyone will be completely happy with communication.

How to get it right

Here are some examples of what you can do in your budget review to try to get it right:

- Agree a communications plan at the beginning of your review, including being clear about any information that should remain confidential.

- Clearly communicate the vision and objectives of your budget review in a way that helps people to understand the context, purpose and need. Be clear about your reasons first so that the message is consistent.

- Help people to understand how the changes will affect them personally. If you don't, people may make up their own stories, which can be sometimes be more negative than the truth.

- Display high-energy and enthusiasm in your communications about your budget review and the changes. People are more likely to respond positively if you are passionate about the subject.

- Communicate as much as possible, soon after the information about the changes becomes available. Share with people that you are aiming for instant communication, which means that some details may change later. The other option is to hold back on information until all aspects are certain. This can be a very ineffective approach to change management which rarely works well in getting people on board.

- Communicate with unions about potential pay budget changes when appropriate. For example, if your budget review leads to a consultation to reduce staff, unions should be invited to discuss the proposals and process and be kept fully informed and given the opportunity to support their members throughout.

- Communicate your budget review changes consistently, frequently and through multiple channels, including speaking, writing, video, training and focus groups as appropriate to the messages.

- Give people time to ask questions and contribute their thoughts and ideas to the changes, so that people feel involved. This will help to create the commitment you need.

- The budget review leader and teams should get out and about and speak to people who are expected to make changes face to face, either one to one or in small groups. Remember true communication is a conversation which is two-way and involves discussion. It can't be just a presentation.

- Only tackle a question if you know the answer. If you don't, go and find out. Providing an answer that turns out to be incorrect is much worse than admitting you don't know. People will have more trust in you, and you will maintain more credibility, if you say you don't know but commit to finding out the answer quickly. Once the information has been gathered, you should make sure you follow up the conversation with the person who asked the question and anyone else who was part of the conversation.

- Communication should be two-way, so make sure you listen more than you speak. Communicate thoughtfully without giving answers too quickly. Don't be defensive or make excuses.

- Make yourself and your teams available amongst staff, and other stakeholders if necessary, so that conversations can take place.

- Ensure communication is proactive and starts early, to prevent rumours circulating before you have started the communication process.

- Provide opportunities for training, including interactive workshops and networking so that colleagues can safely explore the changes together. Staff at every level should be involved in the training, including senior leaders.

The following approach can be a useful communication tool for organisational change. It involves the leader communicating the change by promoting the 'what's in it for the individual or team' as the first priority, 'what's in it for the organisation' as a close second and the potential for financial savings almost as an added bonus. This makes the individual or team feel more important than the need for saving money. This goes a long way to getting people on board rather than making them feel that saving money is the core aim and their feelings or experiences don't matter as much.

What's in it for the individual or team?	Making people's lives easier and saving time.
What's in it for the organisation?	Improving the effectiveness of the organisation to impact positively on outcomes.
Does it reduce waste and save money?	Securing financial savings/reducing waste.

It's also important to remember, when considering 'what's in it for the organisation', that better outcomes for the organisation can often reflect well on an individual or a team. Linking the success of the school as a whole to an individual or team performance will further enhance this change management tool.

Sharing impact, rewarding success

Share with people the effects of the changes as you are going along. Don't wait a year, for example, to share news of the savings that have been made. Positive information, recognition and reward will motivate people to continue with their behavioural changes and encourage others in their area to do so. Recognising and rewarding those doing well publicly, perhaps in staff briefing sessions or meetings, will help to encourage staff to remain on board. It will also maintain the high profile of your budget review and associated changes.

Close the circle on your budget review by reporting back, face to face, the overall savings made over the timeline you have identified. Refer to your original context, purpose and need and share the extent to which the objectives have been met. Where possible, put this into the context of what your school can now do because of these changes. Thank people for their input and contribution to making the changes a success. This will help to maintain positive relationships and get buy-in for the next change management opportunity, of which there may be many in your budget review.

Cultural change to support collaboration

When schools work together to achieve financial efficiency, leadership of change is very important. Some areas of collaborative review may involve background changes which can be carried out relatively easily, without the need for stakeholder involvement and with very little visible impact. An example might be when schools order goods or services in bulk. Discounts can be achieved because the higher volume of purchases brings buying power. Stakeholders will still make use of the same goods or services and will be largely unaware of the process for bringing these into school.

However, if the change impacts on the visible operations of the collaborating schools and the behaviours of stakeholders, then change management once again becomes critical to success. An example of this type of change is when schools work together to share group training hosted by one of the schools. This may be a better value option than each school paying for external trainers individually. Staff from different schools will need to be prepared to work together during the training.

School leaders will also need to work together in their strategic leadership to gain from the benefits of the collaboration. There may be hidden benefits to this type of collaboration which are not realised until the training takes place, such as sharing of good practice, knowledge and skills between schools. Collaboration is one aspect of leadership that can help a school gain an outstanding inspection judgement.

What can make collaborative change more complex is the need to get used to the way another organisation works. In an ideal world, there will be enough similarities and like-minded thinking to make finding a shared way of working fairly straightforward. But it is worth remembering that schools and school leaders do not always work in the same way and some compromise may be needed.

In examples of significant collaboration, before committing to any new ways of working it is useful to establish that the school you are looking to work with is an organisation with similar values to your school. The leaders of each school involved should be like-minded individuals. You should always follow the same principles of financial management, business management and change management as you would if you were working as an individual organisation. Never compromise your core values, or you risk the cost of change being very high.

It is equally as important to manage the cultural change as it is to manage the procedural change when collaborating. You need to tackle both aspects in order for the overall change to be effective. It is all too easy for people to revert back to their normal ways of working, especially if the impetus for change is perceived to be coming from another school. So make sure any changes to systems are properly recorded and understood by everyone using them across the collaborative partnership, and check periodically that they are being adopted as you intended.

Whether working collaboratively with another school or not, communication with appropriate stakeholders at every stage and at all levels is essential for effective change leadership.

12 SYSTEM AND PROCEDURAL CHANGE

Identifying changes

There are many examples of day to day efficiency changes that could result from your budget review which require a system or procedural change. Examples might include:

- how the school is invoiced for telephone bills, resulting in changes to the use of the bank account and alterations to financial procedures.
- how the settings on photocopiers are set up: for example, switching the default to duplex/mono printing to encourage less waste.
- moving from a paper-based system to an electronic system to save staff time, reduce printing and improve on levels of authorisation, for example in relation to requests for cover/absence.
- Introducing into financial procedures a set of rules or guidelines that the finance team should follow for every purchase, to ensure they are getting the best deal.

Steps to take

To manage the change, you need to review what needs to be done and consider the expected impact. Think about the implications of the change and assess any risks, taking care to avoid or minimise them where possible.

To ensure the change is clear, sustainable and easy for others to understand and follow in the future, you need to ensure that changes are recorded, no matter how minor they are.

Do you have an efficient mechanism to update your financial procedures? If your normal practice is an annual update, do you have a working document where changes are added or amended in real time, producing a live up-to-date version that is reviewed as part of your annual update? It would be very difficult to look back at the end of the year and try to remember all the changes that have come about. They may seem significant as they happen, but will you really remember them a year down the line?

Changes to lower-profile procedures or systems also need to be clearly recorded as you make the change. It is particularly important to keep records that explain why a system change has been made. This helps with future review, establishing lessons learnt and what may or may not be done differently in the future. You should always work on the assumption that it might not be the same person who reviews the system in the future, so notes that only you can understand will not do.

The way in which you use technical systems, such as IT systems, should be recorded using a common language, specific to the system, that anyone with the appropriate expertise will be able to understand. It is also useful to build a knowledge database as you review technical areas and find out useful information. This will help with day to day working with the systems, as well as being a significant help in future reviews, whether undertaken by yourself or someone else.

When third parties are involved in, and could alter, systems or procedures that you are changing, you need to be sure you are managing and recording any changes carefully. Whilst you may see the third party as the 'expert', don't believe everything you are told. Check facts and even get a second opinion if you are unsure. Check calculations of expected financial savings and have a mechanism to hold the third party to account, if these savings are not made.

You need to make sure other factors have not impacted on the potential for savings. For example, if a reprographics company promises to reduce the cost per copy and forecasts financial savings at your current usage levels, remember that you might not achieve these savings if your usage levels increase. They are offering a like for like change. The same would be true if the same third party were suggesting an upgrade of machinery which would improve quality and reduce operating costs. Be aware that promises like these do not take volume usage into account. You need to have your own mechanisms for monitoring usage versus cost and quality, to establish whether the change has offered better value for money or not.

Photocopying and printing is an example of a budget area where internal procedural, third party and cultural change could all be evident. If managed carefully, there could be some significant savings to be made. Remember to check what you spend on this budget area in the first place. The budget review leader will have done this when identifying this as an area in need of review, but the teams should understand this aspect too, to understand the significance of the change they are trying to achieve.

When collaborating with other schools, managing and recording system and procedural change is especially important. Two or more organisations may work slightly differently. When common ground is established for the change, a detailed record of procedures needs to be maintained. This will be important if any organisation ever needs to look back on the process, if there are any queries or discrepancies or if the process is likely to be repeated in the future.

In the example of collaborative procurement, one school will need to take the lead in the procurement process and invoice other schools for their contributions. This process should be clearly recorded, providing a full audit trail for scrutiny and review when necessary.

13 OPERATIONAL ACTION PLANS

Planning for specific budget review areas

Teams should already have access to the strategic action plan prepared by the budget review leader. This details the objective to be met for each budget area and the success criteria which will be used to assess whether that objective has been achieved.

The purpose of the operational action plans is to identify the actions that are required to achieve the objective for each budget area. Initially this may be fairly high-level, with wording such as 'investigate the need for...' or 'establish the current level of waste in...'.

As actions are carried out, the detail of the operational action plans should be deepened. Whilst it doesn't have to become a detailed 'to do' list of every task that has been undertaken, it is useful to include as much detail as each team sees fit, to make the plans useful and usable in a practical sense. Actions can then be allocated to individuals within the teams and it becomes easy to keep a track on progress.

The operational action plans are working documents which can change over time to keep pace with whatever may be being unveiled in the review. The objective for the budget area usually remains the same, unless amended by the budget review leader, so this should always be kept in mind as the operational action plans develop.

Teams will undertake the review from the initial actions they have identified, but their review will lead to the formulation of more actions as they go along. The first time a review of a budget area is carried out, teams could be trying different things to establish what is required. If the budget review is carried out again in the future, this record of actions will be a useful starting point and may make future budget reviews quicker, easier and more efficient.

The operational action plans also help the budget review leader to hold the teams to account. The process can be quite detailed and complex depending on the budget area, but it is important to keep the action plans up to date in terms of capacity, timelines, resources and training needs. These requirements should be fed back to the budget review leader via progress updates throughout the process. In the early stages of the review, there will be a lot of unknowns. As more is uncovered, the teams and the budget review leader may need to be responsive to ensure the review stays on track.

Template for a budget review operational action plan

As you can see from our example below, the operational action plans themselves should look similar to a school development plan. We offer a step by step guide in Part 3, which supports the thinking behind the operational action plans and the development of the individual actions, identified risks and risk management strategies. This exercise will guide you in developing the operational action plans.

The operational action plans are internal planning documents which may be shared between the teams and the budget review leader, but are unlikely to be reported more widely. The strategic action plan itself is much more likely to be included in reporting to other stakeholders where necessary, such as governors.

Below is an example of a template you can use for operational action plans for each budget area.

Priority Budget Area:				
Project Team:		Objective:		
Success Criteria:				
Action	Who?	When?	Resources	Monitored by

Part 3: Step by Step Guide to Your Budget Review

14 BUDGET REVIEW MODEL

Planning the review of a budget area

Part 3 is a practical section allowing you to consider some key budget areas which you may need to focus on as part of your budget review. We suggest some prompts and questions which you and your budget review teams can use to explore all aspects of the priority area being examined. The information gleaned from this can then be used to develop the operational action plan for each budget area, enabling the budget review leader to hold the budget review teams to account.

As a starting point, we suggest that each team has some structured planning time to think about the area of the budget they are working on, using the planning template below.

Budget area:	
Why or how might waste/inefficiency occur?	
•	
What can be done to improve efficiency?	What is the process for making this happen?
•	•
Are there any risks in making the changes?	How can risk be reduced or eliminated?
•	•
What is the expected impact of the change?	

When this exercise is complete, the information will be invaluable in developing the operational action plan, using the template demonstrated at the end of the previous chapter. Each team will then have a clear list of tasks to undertake, in order to complete the budget review in their area.

The detail in the planning template provides an excellent basis to form the actions that the team needs to carry out. Remember to consider all the risks you have identified and ways to minimise these when you are formulating your operational action plan.

Examples of review plans

In the next chapter, we will show you what this planning exercise might look like for a selection of budget areas. Our list of examples is not exhaustive, but gives a good range that you might be likely to come across in your budget review.

We have grouped some similar budget areas together to allow you to apply our practical advice across a variety of scenarios. We have also considered some commonly-used management accounting categories, to give you a full flavour of what is possible in your budget review.

As you read each planning template, think about your own school context. We have posed questions to you as the budget review leader to guide you in your thinking. To use our examples as a template, tailor the wording to make it appropriate to your audience. Reflect on whether you see similarities in your own setting and whether the steps we suggest can be transferred directly to your review. You may find that the steps you need to take differ, but the overall approach can offer you guidance on how to tackle each area.

The example budget areas we have chosen are:
1) Pay budgets
2) Cleaning Arrangements and Grounds Maintenance
3) IT services
4) Data Management
5) Support contracts, including equipment maintenance
6) Supply
7) Telephony
8) Printing and photocopying
9) IT Equipment/Consumables/IT Refresh
10) Special Educational Needs & Disabilities (SEND)
11) Behaviour and Attendance

Often the first step is the hardest, so let's get started.

15 REVIEWING PAY BUDGETS

An example of a pay budget review plan

Your pay budget makes up the biggest proportion of your overall budget and should therefore be the starting point in any review to ensure that VfM is achieved and that you can make financial savings. With budgets of significant size such as this, even seemingly small changes can have a big impact and resulting savings can be of high value. No matter how lean or efficient you believe your staffing structures to be, it is likely that some improvements can be made.

Once you have undergone your first budget review in this area, regular review, ideally on an annual basis, will ensure you are using your resources to best effect and maximising the impact of your staff on pupil outcomes.

For pay budgets we have provided a VfM assessment checklist in chapter 4. We will consider here the actions that might arise from your answers to a few of the questions across the economy, efficiency, effectiveness and leadership structure sections of that checklist. These are only intended to be examples; you will be able to develop your own prompts for other questions that are particularly relevant to your own context.

Budget area: Pay Budgets
Why or how might waste/inefficiency occur?
a. Staff are paid at a higher level than their performance warrants and are not held to account adequately for their performance.
b. Staff are not focused and waste time on tasks that have little or no positive impact on outcomes.
c. Staff are not appropriately trained to undertake their roles effectively.
d. Staffing structures are over-generous and are not a true

reflection of the organisation's needs.

e. Staff redundancy and/or early retirement settlements are paid at an enhanced rate without due consideration for whether this is appropriate.

What can be done to improve efficiency?	What is the process for making this happen?
a. Ensure your appraisal policy and implementation of it are rigorous and robust, to support performance related pay and ensure there is no upward movement when performance does not warrant it.	a. Review policy. Research and compare your appraisal policy against other schools' policies and guidance or templates provided by your LA or Trust. Ensure your policy defines what is meant by key terms in a meaningful way that can be used in practical terms as you implement the policy. For example, define what is meant by 'exceptional' performance. What does this mean? Is it directly related to external examination results or the levels of progress learners make? How do you define 'sustained performance'? Does this equate to a minimum of two years or even longer? Policy implementation: Ensure you have the most appropriate leaders holding staff to account within a defined appraisal structure. Appropriate training is critical to ensure that evaluation of evidence is accurate, consistent and in line with your policy. All staff should have a clear understanding of what constitutes appropriate evidence to support their appraisal review. Appraisers should be confident that the recommendations they put forward for any movement up the pay scale, or not, are backed up with appropriate evidence. The appraisal process itself should be systematic with all information and evidence from meetings clearly recorded and records maintained for scrutiny by the Headteacher and governing board as required. The Headteacher will consider recommendations from the appraisers, but

	the governing board will ultimately approve (or not approve) the recommendations made by the Headteacher. Evidence must be available, accessible, organised and clear.
b. Ensure staff are deployed efficiently to get the most output from their working time.	b. Review staff deployment, accounting for their time and impact. Time: For teaching staff, consider the proportion of their time spent teaching compared to non-contact time, taking into account time for leadership and management duties. Ensure DfE and union guidelines are considered. For support staff, ensure that detailed job descriptions translate to daily, weekly, termly etc. tasks and that appropriate line managers hold team members to account for their work output and productivity. Impact: For teaching staff, consider the impact their time spent has on pupil outcomes using performance data and other measures where appropriate. For support staff, ensure strong line management, coaching and a support staff development review system are all in place to hold staff to account for the impact their contribution has on pupil outcomes and the priorities of the school.
c. Ensure professional development is recorded and evaluated to assess its impact and inform future decisions on training opportunities for all.	c. Assign responsibility for monitoring and recording professional development to a specific member of staff or team. Record, monitor and evaluate all professional development opportunities including external courses and conferences, in-house training sessions, mentoring, coaching and private study.
d. Compare your leadership structure	d. Undertake an initial review which includes financial benchmarking and

to other similar sized schools with a similar profile of need. What does it tell you? Are there legitimate reasons for any difference? If your leadership structure is generous, has this built up over many years? Is it an inherited issue?	other statistical comparisons against similar sized schools with a similar profile. If the result is that your leadership structure appears to be overly generous, consider the reasons why. Are they justifiable? If not, consider a staff consultation to review the leadership structure. Could the consultation result in voluntary redundancy or voluntary relinquishment of some leadership responsibility to re-align your structure and reduce costs? Be aware that entitlement to protection may cause a delay in savings being achieved.
e. Avoid any enhancements to settlements at redundancy or early retirement that might be custom and practice.	e. Review policies on settlements for redundancy or early retirement. Ensure you abide by any relevant regulations. Ensure policies are an appropriate reflection of current practice, not historic practice.
Are there any risks in making the changes?	**How can risk be reduced or eliminated?**
a. Minimal risk (risk occurs if your policy is not robust).	a. N/A
b. Negative impact on staff morale if they feel they are being checked up on or accused of not working hard enough.	b. Conduct discussions with line managers about their teams as part of overall quality assurance, rather than raising directly with individual members of staff. If individual conversations are necessary, explore any deployment issues sensitively, establish reasons for any spare capacity and assess willingness to make a change. Be aware of job descriptions, levels of responsibility, pay grades, how school expectations have been communicated and any special circumstances. If you have an HR team in school, they could lead this review

			using their knowledge and experience of employment law and working regulations to underpin their actions.
c.	Person recording the information does not have sufficient knowledge or teaching and learning leadership experience to evaluate effectively the training to inform future decisions.	c.	If the information is recorded by an admin clerk or member of the HR team, it would be useful to have a senior leader with a teaching and learning overview to contribute to or even lead the discussion on evaluation and impact of training.
d.	Impact on staff morale (particularly leaders) which could impact negatively on their day to day effectiveness and disrupt the operations of the school. Cost of a restructure in the first year when a part year salary plus redundancy costs could be borne by the school. Takes time to bring to conclusion to re-establish the effective running of the whole team.	d.	Seek professional HR advice to ensure all procedures are correctly followed. Transparent correspondence, including face to face meetings with relevant union representatives to ensure the needs of all staff involved in the process are met and that they have independent advice. Clearly communicate and justify the reasons for the consultation detailing the potential impact on pupils and their outcomes, with and without the proposed change.
e.	Impact on staff morale for those approaching settlement who are aware of historic practice.	e.	Clearly communicate changes to all stakeholders (including unions), at the proposal, approval and implementation stages with clear acknowledgment of the date when the changes will be introduced.

JULIE CORDINER & NIKOLA FLINT

What is the expected impact of the change?

a. Staff are paid at the correct level related to their performance, ensuring that the impact they have on student outcomes is reflected in the cost of their employment to the school (VfM).

b. Staff time is suitably deployed to ensure maximum impact on student outcomes and no employees are under-used, which can also have a detrimental effect on morale of other individuals within the team.

c. Most future training decisions are made based on strong evaluation evidence to increase the probability of training effectiveness and a positive impact on student outcomes. It is less likely that money is spent on training which is ineffective.

d. A long-term reduction in leadership costs releases funding to be allocated to better effect, impacting favourably on student outcomes. A leadership structure of appropriate size for the size of the school, with focused roles and responsibilities, drives the school's priorities for improvement.

e. Staff are paid appropriate settlement amounts for redundancy and early retirement.

16 REVIEWING NON-PAY BUDGETS

Cleaning and Grounds Maintenance

In this chapter, we suggest a range of examples of different services or contracts which can be reviewed using the template already referred to. The first area is Cleaning and Grounds Maintenance.

These areas of the budget are particularly important, as the appearance of the school buildings and site contributes significantly to how successfully you can market the school to your stakeholders. If buildings appear to be unclean and unkempt or external areas overgrown and uncared for, this could impact negatively on people's perceptions of your school and may even contribute to a reduction in admissions and ultimately falling pupil rolls. This, in turn, affects funding and does not promote financial health or the culture of value for money that you are working towards.

Planning and undertaking a review of these areas will help to ensure that money is spent wisely to maintain and present your facilities to your best advantage and that, in the long-term, future pupil numbers and associated funding is secured.

Budget area: Cleaning and Grounds Maintenance
Why or how might waste/inefficiency occur?
a. The overall cost of the service does not reflect the quality or quantity of work done.
b. Tasks are carried out more frequently than necessary.
c. Those undertaking the tasks are not held to account for the efficient and effective use of their time, resulting in a culture which is lax and not purposeful.
d. Quality assurance checks are not undertaken, resulting in a poor quality of work.

What can be done to improve efficiency?	What is the process for making this happen?
a. Negotiate service contract costs using the four principles of Best Value (challenge, compare, consult and compete).	a. When establishing a new service contract, compare several providers. When undertaking an annual review of cost, monitor the market for ongoing comparisons and ensure any price increases can be justified to your satisfaction by the service provider. If you employ staff to provide this service in-house, compare your staffing and associated costs with potential contracts to ensure this approach represents value for money.
b. Ensure the service schedule agreed for each month is a true reflection of need and is not over-generous or insufficient in terms of frequency of task. For example, are the toilets being cleaned too often, wasting money? Or is the frequency not often enough or at the wrong times of day, resulting in extra cleans being required?	b. Work with your service provider to review every task within the service schedule. If you are unsure about what is appropriate for your school, suggest a trial period and then review the frequency to increase, decrease or change timings as necessary. Remember you are the customer, so if your provider wants to keep your business they should be accommodating, establishing a service which meets the needs of the school.
c. Ensure adequate management of service staff by the service provider.	c. Ask questions during the set-up of the service about how the service provider intends to manage the team on the ground. Will managers visit the school? How frequently?
d. Ensure regular quality assurance checks and reporting methods.	d. Ensure the service provider carries out regular checks on quality of work undertaken. Agree this when the service is first set up, but don't be afraid to re-

	visit the issue if you have concerns. Carry out your own quality assurance checks and ensure there is an agreed protocol between the school and the service provider to report any concerns regarding working practices. Be aware of any penalty clauses in the contract for under-performance and ensure that your monitoring is able to provide sufficient evidence to invoke the penalties if applicable.
Are there any risks in making the changes?	**How can risk be reduced or eliminated?**
• The member of school staff managing the service contract for the school does not have adequate capacity or the appropriate skill set to manage it effectively, resulting in a poor service and no assurance of value for money.	• Assign the responsibility to a member of staff who has sufficient capacity and an appropriate skill set. If you are a big school or a Trust and there are a number of service contracts to be managed, there may be a need for a specific role for this purpose. Often the SBL or Premises Manager or both will undertake this responsibility. The skills required include negotiation, communication and sometimes specialist knowledge of the service area. Ensure the member of staff with this responsibility is offered adequate support and challenge via their line manager.

What is the expected impact of the change?

The arrangements in place for the service area represent value for money, having been:
- procured at an appropriate cost
- efficiently deployed
- quality assured for effectiveness.

The learning environment effectively supports school organisation, staff and student well-being and the school's priorities for improvement.

IT Services

Schools of all types and phases find themselves with a variety of IT service support set-ups. With the introduction of Building Schools for the Future, some secondary schools found themselves facing fully managed IT service contracts, usually for a period of around 5 years. Some of these schools may still be within those contracts or have chosen to keep a fully managed service. Others may have continued with a partially managed service and some may have moved away from this approach to implement an in-house service where all IT technical staff are directly employed by the school again.

Other schools have also experienced a variety of contexts, from their own in-house service solutions to LA managed services and even third-party outsourcing solutions.

Whatever your context, this budget area often involves substantial sums of money. Moreover, the impact of the school's IT service on the quality of teaching and learning, and ultimately pupil outcomes, cannot be underestimated. The infrastructure needs to support the choice of hardware, software and other technologies adopted in the school's IT road map. The overall IT strategy, including device choice, how children learn, how staff teach and work, and the links between school working and home working, needs to be inspired by and integrated with the teaching and learning vision of the school. Most importantly, in the context of the IT service budget, it all has to work with as little downtime and disruption to learning and working as possible.

Staff expect IT to work reliably, so that they can deliver their lessons and fulfil the school's purpose. Pupils expect IT to work on demand, so that they can learn. Parents expect to hear that the equipment they were promised for their child's education is available and in good working condition. Anything less is not deemed acceptable and a poorly performing IT service can receive very negative attention from staff, parents and pupils alike.

With so much to consider and so many complexities, this is one of the more difficult areas of your budget to review. Where possible, you should ensure that team members reviewing this area have some technical expertise to understand and interpret the issues.

Budget area: IT Services

Why or how might waste/inefficiency occur?
• The overall cost of the service may not reflect the quality of service or the needs of the school. This could apply to an in-house service or an outsourced service which could be partially or fully managed by a third party.

• If in-house:
Staff may not be:
- paid at the right grade for their level of responsibility
- efficiently deployed
- appropriately trained
- effectively managed to get the best out of them
and systems may not:
   - be appropriate for use
   - represent value for money.

• If outsourced:
   - the partly or fully managed service contract may not meet the needs of the school in full
   - delivery of the partly or fully managed service contract may not be high quality, hence may not be having the desired impact on school operations, student outcomes and school priorities.

What can be done to improve efficiency?	**What is the process for making this happen?**

Review which set-up is best for your school and undergo a change process to implement the most suitable option:
  • In-house IT service
  • Partially managed IT service
  • Fully managed IT service.
If you are already working within the set-up that you believe to be the most suitable for your school, but you feel
	Prepare an IT service business plan which explores all available options and considers the school context to inform decisions for IT service set-up.
	The success of an in-house IT service is reliant on a team with sufficient spread of competence, expertise and skill to deal with the majority of scenarios a school can expect to face. External expertise can still be sought, but this should be the exception rather than the rule, otherwise you may be spending more than necessary in employing your own staff and buying in external expertise.
	If you are a big school or work as part of a Trust, an in-house IT service may be the most favourable option because of the capacity you can create. This can often be a cheaper method of achieving a quality service

the service is inefficient, review all aspects and make changes where appropriate.	which is highly professional, generally more bespoke to the school(s) and more flexible to suit need. If the most favourable option is to outsource your IT service requirements to a third party, consider the contract and its delivery as part of your efficiency review: a. Is the specification appropriate for the needs of your school? Have the school's needs changed? Can the contract be adapted to reflect changes in need? b. Does the cost of the contract reflect the level of service delivered? Use benchmarking to compare the cost of solutions implemented by other similar schools. c. Are there quality assurance processes in place, to ensure that delivery of the contract is to an agreed standard? Are the Key Performance Indicators (KPIs) used to measure performance appropriate? Do they work in favour of the contractor, i.e. always met but with the school feeling the level of service is inadequate? Can KPIs be reviewed and changed? What is the process for this? When can it happen? d. If the level of service is not deemed adequate, what is the process for ending the contract? Are there any penalty clauses for early release?
Are there any risks in making the changes?	**How can risk be reduced or eliminated?**
In-house: • Do you have sufficient capacity and expertise to lead and develop a team with a sufficient spread of competence,	In-house • Recruitment • Training • Reference visits to schools who do this well (school-to-school support) • Supervision arrangements.

expertise and skill?	
Outsourced: • Do you have the expertise within your teams to identify the best service provider and negotiate a contract? Can you produce an accurate specification for the contract that ensures it will meet the needs of your school? An IT service contract is a big commitment of funds, especially if the contract exceeds one year.	Outsourced: • Consider working with an independent consultant/specialist or accessing school-to-school support to guide your staff to undergo this process effectively.

What is the expected impact of the change?

- A cost-effective solution that represents value for money.
- IT infrastructure, systems, hardware and software operate smoothly with minimal disruption to learning.
- The IT service is flexible to meet changing school need and is a key driver for broader change management to support the development of teaching and learning and school operations.
- In-house teams offer both technical and developmental IT support and may support other school teams in areas such as website and marketing and design services. There may be links to other teams in school to support data consolidation and effective system design, management and use to support the wider context of school operations.

Data Management

The volume, variety and complexity of data that schools are responsible for is growing rapidly. The need for complex management information systems with sophisticated functionality has never been higher. It is common for schools to perceive that they need to invest more funds in this area to keep up with the demands placed on them, especially in response to new regulations such as GDPR (General Data Protection Regulations). See our guest blog post by Paul Norris, Principal Consultant at Infinity Consultancy Ltd at https://schoolfinancialsuccess.com/gdpr-helping-you-to-be-prepared/.

Far too often, investment in data systems is done in a reactive and ad-hoc manner to deal with each individual issue as it arises. This can result in a number of systems running alongside each other with no real integration or communication between them.

A budget review of this area will encourage a review of your overall data management strategy, as well as systems, and could lead to an overall solution which better represents value for money.

Budget area: Data Management
Why or how might waste/inefficiency occur?
• Multiple school systems, not intelligently linked, resulting in numerous ad hoc spreadsheets and databases which cause inefficient working practices.   • Pupil data not accurately recorded or maintained, resulting in inaccurate funding and poor analysis of outcomes, leading to missed opportunities to support under-achieving groups and improve standards of attainment overall.   • Insufficient understanding of unit costs and the behaviour of costs (fixed, stepped and variable) which could result in inefficient deployment of staff, inaccurate cost interpretation and poor contract management.   • Lack of awareness of changing regulations, such as General Data Protection Regulations (GDPR).

What can be done to improve efficiency?	What is the process for making this happen?
• Consolidate IT systems where appropriate, eliminating ad hoc spreadsheets and databases to improve efficiency. • Keep up to date with potential changes to regulations, to inform strategic planning for data	• Identify system overlaps and dependencies by auditing all systems in use, mapping their purpose and content. • Automate processes wherever possible. • Ensure key systems work intelligently together and are cross-fertilised with accurate and real-time information. • Research the changes and sources of support. Undertake an audit of your current position in relation to new regulations and formulate an action plan to achieve compliance. Consider

	how all data systems and processes inter-relate for maximum efficiency and to ensure compliance.
Are there any risks in making the changes?	**How can risk be reduced or eliminated?**
• Existing staff teams may not be competent to make improvements to the required level in this complex area, or may actively resist the changes.	• Ensure staff using systems are properly trained, competent and given sufficient time to carry out processes accurately. • Assign a highly competent senior leader role with an appropriate level of understanding and skill set to oversee strategic data management and facilitate changes in this area. • Seek external expert support to establish new ways of working that can then be maintained by existing staff. • Identify champions to encourage and support reluctant peers.

What is the expected impact of the change?

- A cost-effective solution that represents value for money.
- A co-ordinated and consolidated data management set-up that minimises the need for isolated systems and uses automated processes wherever possible.
- Well trained, competent and effective staff who can utilise the data systems to their full potential and suggest continual improvements in response to change.
- An efficient and effective data management system which supports the strategic use of data to inform all aspects of school life including, for example, behaviour management, attendance and student progress.

Support contracts including equipment maintenance

Schools are far more likely to be successful if teaching and learning is not disrupted by building or equipment faults. When this happens on a regular basis, it can have a significant detrimental impact on student outcomes and, in the worst-case scenarios, can result in a temporary school closure, resulting in learning days lost and a poor perception of the school by stakeholders, in particular parents.

Support contracts are necessary for various types of equipment for the following main reasons:

- To support health and safety compliance, ensuring that vital equipment is maintained and tested, with all appropriate actions taken to prevent fault or breakdown. This approach supports schools in their efforts to avoid the disruption to learning that a temporary school closure would cause.
- To promote financial efficiency. It is often more economical to pay for a support contract, which can include repair costs or reduced rates, rather than paying a higher price which may be charged to customers without a support contract.

Of course, it might not be in a school's interests to enter into a support contract at all, or to embark upon one without due consideration of the details of the contract. It is an area that schools need to be very savvy about, assessing each support contract thoroughly, on its own merit and from every angle.

Budget area: Support Contracts
Why or how might waste/inefficiency occur?
<ul><li>The contract does not reflect school need and includes more or less than is actually required.</li><li>The contract reflects school need on paper, but in practice the agreed tasks are not carried out to the agreed frequency or at the desired quality.</li><li>Support contracts are no longer required by the school but are still in place because they have never been reviewed, or because action was not taken early enough to terminate or alter the contract.</li><li>The contract is over-priced.</li></ul>

What can be done to improve efficiency?	What is the process for making this happen?
• Ensure contracts reflect school need.	• Ensure accurate specifications are drawn up to reflect the school's needs. Obtain legal support and advice where necessary. • Review contracts for appropriateness at the time of set-up and as part of the annual review before renewal. Allocate at least two staff members to contribute to this evaluation, including one with specific knowledge of the service area or specialist equipment and one with skills in contract review. • If a support contract is no longer required, be aware of the actions and timeline required to terminate the contract. Make contact with the supplier early to put the mechanism to terminate in motion. This will avoid unwanted renewal or penalty clauses. • Similarly, if a contract requires some alteration to ensure school need is reflected, be aware of the process for doing so and action changes as soon as you know they are required.
• Quality assure contract work.	• Assign the most appropriate staff member(s) to undertake quality assurance checks of contract work undertaken. This does not necessarily have to be the staff who were involved in contract set-up/review, but they should maintain an overview of the ongoing success of the contract and remain fully informed in readiness for the next review. • Understand and implement the mechanism for reporting poor quality to the supplier and holding them to account. Assign this responsibility to the most appropriate member of staff and ensure an internal line of reporting to the Headteacher, should any issue need to be escalated.

• Maintain a contracts calendar.	• Assign to a member of staff the responsibility for creating and maintaining a calendar which clearly details supplier details, contract purpose, start date, end date and action required to renew/terminate contract. The calendar should be distributed to any member of staff with responsibility to carry out any action at any stage of the process. One person should hold all staff involved to account to ensure there is a co-ordinated approach to all support contract management.
• Compare costs/prices to ensure the best deal.	• Proactively contact each supplier well in advance and pursue discounts/loyalty bonuses for early sign up. • Use financial benchmarking tools and your professional network to compare costs and prices. National deals are available in the DfE's buying strategy at https://www.gov.uk/government/publications/schools-buying-strategy. • Local comparisons are often useful within your local schools' network. Negotiate the best deals and compare more than one supplier.
Are there any risks in making the changes?	**How can risk be reduced or eliminated?**
• Member of staff undertaking quality assurance is not suitably qualified/skilled to do so.	• Assign a staff member with knowledge related to the contract purpose where possible. Consider training if there is a skills gap amongst the team. Seek external support from LA or within your Trust or trusted network if necessary. • Assign a highly competent senior leader role with an appropriate level of understanding and skill set to oversee strategic data management and facilitate changes in this area. • Seek external expert support to establish new ways of working that can then be maintained by existing staff.

	• Identify champions to encourage and support reluctant peers.
• Contract invoices are paid despite quality not being acceptable.	• Ensure payment is linked to a quality assurance process and that where you have concerns, invoices are formally disputed with the supplier until issues are resolved. Invoke penalty clauses if appropriate.
• Can be time-consuming to undertake every part of the process well.	• Ensure capacity and time is built in to achieve a thorough process.

What is the expected impact of the change?

The school is health and safety compliant, taking preventative action rather than reacting to events after they have occurred. It holds contracts which truly reflect the school's need and offer high quality support. Learning is not disrupted and student outcomes are not threatened.

The school gets the best deal in terms of cost and quality, representing value for money.

Supply teaching

This area of expenditure directly impacts on teaching and learning and is therefore an extremely important area of consideration. If not well managed and carefully planned, pupils may end up with a poor deal, with a cover solution which threatens their continued progress and chances of academic success. The most important consideration from a teaching and learning perspective is that the best possible person is teaching the class at all times. This is often a competing demand with the need to ensure value for money, as cover solutions can be very costly.

There are several steps which can be taken to assess your current cover management and make improvements if necessary. Schools use a number of different creative approaches, some of which work in some schools and not in others. Understanding the context of your school, including the phase-specific context and the profile of your staff and students, is a very important consideration when reviewing your processes and procedures for this area of the budget.

Budget area: Supply teaching	
Why or how might waste/inefficiency occur?	
• Poor absence management processes. • Inefficient use of external supply agencies. • Lack of strategic planning.	
What can be done to improve efficiency?	**What is the process for making this happen?**
• Ensure absence management processes are robust.	• Ensure authoriser roles are in place to restrict requests for cover when it is avoidable or not appropriate. Ideally this should be a senior leader with a good overview of all aspects of school life to inform decision making. • Ensure appropriate budgets are used to cover external supply costs. A process should be in place between the finance team and cover manager. Consider the best way of reporting spending, e.g. linking the external supply budget with the teaching budget for a holistic view. • Establish an effective process for communication and feedback between staff, authorisers and the cover manager. This could include a digital system for absence requests to make the process more efficient, but should not replace the need for face to face communication, as this is about people and their lives. • Thoroughly check invoices from supply agencies against time sheets and internal records to ensure accuracy. Challenge any discrepancies sooner rather than later. • Give staff the means to report planned and unplanned staff absence efficiently and in a timely manner.
• Use external supply agency services intelligently.	• Consider balancing the use of external supply agencies with direct employment of floating teachers/cover supervisors. This can be more cost effective and

	brings other benefits such as bespoke training to meet the school's needs, consistency and relationship building with pupils and staff. • Negotiate daily and half-day rates to ensure they represent value for money. Compare with other agencies; there is a lot of competition. • If the quality of personnel provided is not satisfactory, do not be afraid to report your feedback to the agency (you are the customer) and trial the use of other agencies if quality does not improve.
• Strategically plan your approach to staff absence management.	• Prevention is better than cure. Analyse and interpret absence data to inform staff well-being programmes. • Build a culture where staff want to be in school because they feel rewarded for the positive impact they have on the pupils in their care. • Ensure efficient data systems are available to support better planning for the use of supply. • Encourage staff to make medical/dental appointments outside of school hours and promote local healthcare providers who offer this service. • Provide services for staff in school such as regular health checks. • Consider whether staff absence insurance is cost effective for the school. Is it likely that the expected reimbursements will exceed the cost of the premium, and what will the impact of the policy be on staff?
Are there any risks in making the changes?	**How can risk be reduced or eliminated?**
• Cover supervisors directly employed by the school could be	• Introduce or review staff well-being programmes.

absent due to sickness.	
• Staff absence insurance policies may require invasive questioning of staff for medical details before a claim can be accepted. This may have a negative impact on staff well-being. • The processes for claiming may place a heavy demand on administrative staff time.	• Understand exactly what the set-up and claim process will entail before signing up to a policy.

What is the expected impact of the change?
Higher quality of cover personnel results in a positive impact on pupil outcomes, with greater assurance of continued progress even in the absence of their specialist teacher. Financial savings are achieved through reduced absence, more cost-effective use of directly employed staff, better value rates for external supply and potentially reimbursements from staff absence insurance.

Telephony

Telephony remains one of the key methods of communication for schools. The safety and safeguarding of pupils is the most important consideration for all schools; when telephone lines go down, it can cause significant issues.

Parents need to know they can make contact with the school easily, to exchange important information about their child when necessary. Recognising the importance of this commodity, many schools have invested in telephony solutions to ensure reliability and a high quality and efficient service.

Modern-day systems bring with them a certain level of complexity which can make it more difficult for schools to keep track of how well their system provides value for money. Providers are often difficult to contact and it can be off-putting for school staff who are investigating potential improvements to their system set-up.

Perseverance can and does pay off. For schools whose telephony charges are significant, it is very likely that there will be some savings to be made with no cultural change required for staff and minimal impact on parents and other stakeholders, if managed well.

Budget area: Telephony	
Why or how might waste/inefficiency occur?	
• Telecommunications provider may not be offering value for money in the contract. • Line set-up may not be a true reflection of school need, resulting in excessive line rental charges. • Payment logistics may not be efficient enough to meet providers' payment terms and may result in late payment charges. • Missed opportunities to make savings via Direct Debit (DD) payments rather than the more traditional paper invoicing system. • Excessive call usage, over and above genuine school business need.	
What can be done to improve efficiency?	**What is the process for making this happen?**
• Ensure VfM is achieved in contract negotiations and consider changing provider if necessary.	• Review all related contracts simultaneously, e.g. telephony and broadband, in case there are savings to be made from a single provider.
• Review line set-up against school need.	• Make sure bills are itemised and that every line you are paying for is justified. Demand an on-site visit by the provider if necessary, to resolve any queries and establish what the set-up is. This will provide you with the information you need in order to measure your school's need and make important decisions which could save you money.
• Establish the most cost-effective way to pay for the service and make it happen.	• Payment terms and conditions for telephony providers tend to be 14 days or fewer, which can cause problems for schools working with a paper invoice system. Depending on staffing capacity, this can become a bigger issue during school holiday periods. • Schools with their own bank accounts

	(including cheque book schools) should have no barriers to paying by Direct Debit (DD), removing the issue of late payment. It may also lead to the identification of savings in other areas of your budget. Non-cheque book schools should investigate solutions with the LA, who should try to be accommodating in the interests of school financial efficiency.
• Establish if there is a cultural issue in your school relating to call usage. Does usage represent a genuine school business need?	• Undertake financial benchmarking to compare your telephony charges against similar-sized schools with similar characteristics. Do you feel you have a reason to analyse information any further? If so… • Analyse billing information to understand how your charges are made up. If usage charges are high or higher than you would expect, do you have a telephone system that can analyse usage to identify where calls are made from in the school? Are there any obvious anomalies? Are calls being made abroad that you wouldn't expect? The likelihood is that call charges will represent a legitimate school need, but it is good practice to have an overview to establish if this is the case and not just assume that it is. Is there a serious cultural issue that you are aware of? What messages can you give to set expectations of staff behaviour?
Are there any risks in making the changes?	**How can risk be reduced or eliminated?**
• This could be a time-consuming exercise. You are in the hands of the telephony provider who	• Try to get a feel for potential savings, starting with how much you spend on telephony. If this is a very small amount, you won't want a team of

may or may not work at the speed you would like. Do you foresee savings being worth the time spent?	staff spending months working on a review to make hundreds of pounds of savings. If you think there is scope to save thousands of pounds, you are more likely to proceed with the review.
• Use of a Direct Debit facility on your bank account may contravene audit regulations due to the nature of auto-renew style payments and the freedom for the provider to take an amount directly from your bank account without prior authorisation of the exact amount.	• Establish a timely and thorough check of the DD payment, enabling any challenge to the provider to be made promptly after the DD payment has left the bank. Systems such as 'onebill' from BT provide an easily identifiable breakdown which can be manually checked as part of a regular procedure. Record the procedure you will undergo in your Financial Procedures Manual and ensure that staff carrying out the procedure are fully trained, competent and that a second layer of checks is in place.

What is the expected impact of the change?
Financial savings with little or no cultural impact. These are likely to be background changes which are not widely visible to stakeholders and do not impact on their behaviours. Efficient telephony systems which represent good value for money and provide resilience in case of emergencies.

Printing and photocopying

Printing and photocopying are still key communication tools for many schools, although for some their reliance on this area is diminishing as new technologies and communication methods are explored and used to better effect. The transition is not straightforward, with a significant potential impact on cultural change and people's day to day behaviours. This is a key budget area to review, with great potential for improved efficiency. The benefits of improvements are three-fold and are all relevant to your budget review.

Firstly, there are financial savings to be made if the volume of printing and photocopying is reduced, either from a reduction in waste, the opportunity to use alternative methods or a combination of both.

Secondly, the desired impact or effectiveness of what is being communicated may be improved using a different method. Digital technologies allow for anytime/anywhere access for example, and can also mean that parents and carers have access to information and resources directly from school staff, without relying on pupils to share this with them.

Finally, the impact of making improvements in this area on the value for money culture you are striving for should not be underestimated. The messages people receive and understand in making changes to their behaviours in this area will translate to all aspects of their work, reminding them of the value of resources and their accountability for the use of public funds.

Pupils also benefit from cultural change in this area, particularly if they have access to their own printing accounts which is often the case, especially for secondary aged pupils. Learning the importance of efficiency, respect for their environment and how their individual actions impact on the whole community are all important lessons to prepare them for the world of work.

Budget area: Printing and Photocopying	
Why or how might waste/inefficiency occur?	
Printing and photocopying is done without proper consideration of questions such as: • Is it needed? • Is there another method of achieving the same result, e.g. digital communication? • Does it need to be in colour or black and white (mono)? • Does it need to be single sided (simplex) or double sided (duplex)? • How many copies are needed? • Which devices in the school are used? The overall printing strategy does not ensure that: • the equipment in the school is fit for purpose • staff are properly trained and educated in the efficient use of the equipment • there is adequate monitoring of printing/photocopying accounts, to hold staff to account and inform future strategy.	
What can be done to improve efficiency?	**What is the process for making this happen?**
• Develop a printing/photocopying strategy and implement it.	• Educate staff in the most efficient use of the equipment available. Do you have different types of printing devices in school? Are some more

	financially efficient than others? Are some types of jobs better suited to some types of equipment than others? If possible and necessary, configure your IT system with some restrictions which push certain jobs to the more efficient equipment. If you are not comfortable with this, empower staff and pupils with the knowledge and information to make these decisions for themselves. Ensure a robust usage monitoring system is in place to hold people to account. • Educate staff in alternative solutions such as digital communication, where appropriate. Offer staff support from IT teams in use of alternative technologies.
• Ensure equipment is fit for purpose and runs efficiently.	• Invite your provider in to review and evaluate your current equipment set-up, offering advice and guidance to ensure your solution meets your school's needs.
• Review contracts to ensure best value.	• Compare print solutions with different suppliers to establish which set-up would work best for your school. Older, less efficient devices can mean that a 'cost per copy' charge is higher. Check all details of proposals and contracts including cost per copy charges and leasing arrangements.
Are there any risks in making the changes?	**How can risk be reduced or eliminated?**
• Contracts can be confusing and often make assumptions about usage when forecasting expected costs.	• Make sure you understand the unit costs being proposed and that you apply them to your expected usage to get a more probable picture of the overall cost to the school. • Get expert advice on leasing arrangements before you sign up.

• If you are making changes to the level of freedom you give to your staff, it may impact negatively on staff morale.	• Consider all aspects of cultural change management when implementing any changes. If you are aiming for a change in people's behaviours, this should be managed very carefully, to sell the change and get buy-in from the outset and throughout.

What is the expected impact of the change?

Staff have adequate knowledge and training to:
- apply sound judgement of when to print and photocopy and when to use other forms of communication, i.e. digital communication
- use the available equipment efficiently.

Monitoring is robust, detailed and informs future strategy as well as providing information to managers to hold users to account.

Photocopying and printing costs are reduced.

IT: equipment, consumables and refresh

Staff, pupils and other stakeholders in schools usually expect IT equipment to just work. The complicated technical world behind the devices and infrastructure many of us use on a day to day basis is baffling to many people and sparks little interest.

Essentially, teachers want reassurance that the lesson they have planned will go off without a technical hitch. All staff want to know that their individual devices will work effectively, and allow them to achieve their daily tasks without hindrance. Like the ball boys and girls at Wimbledon, when it goes well it is not noticed, but when it goes wrong, it is all that is talked about.

The impact on teaching and learning of a failing IT service or equipment is significant in the short-term and can be devastating over the medium to long-term. More and more schools rely on digital systems for data management, safeguarding, attendance and behaviour and the delivery of teaching and learning, including the use of pupil planners and communications with parents. IT is now the backbone of our school organisation and must be fit for purpose and reliable to support the school's success.

For those working in IT in schools, the challenges are substantial, but much can be done to prevent failure and reduce inefficiency.

Budget area: IT equipment, consumables and refresh

Why or how might waste/inefficiency occur?

- IT equipment or consumables:
  - are over priced
  - are not high quality
  - do not impact positively on learning
  - are not used, or not used effectively.
- The programme for IT Refresh:
  - does not meet school need
  - is not affordable
  - is not co-ordinated across the school
  - does not impact positively on learning
  - is not a rolling programme and does not keep up with the changing face of technology
  - does not account for changing regulations such as GDPR (General Data Protection Regulation)
  - does not take account of changing school context such as increasing or decreasing pupil numbers.

What can be done to improve efficiency?	What is the process for making this happen?
• Maintain a central asset register and audit the current use of IT equipment.	• A central team (IT Technical team if you run an in-house service) should undertake this task and ensure it is constantly up to date. If you outsource your service, this may be included in the contract.

• Evaluate impact.	• In consultation with those who use the equipment, judge the impact it has and record it. Use data to inform your judgement.
	• What is the impact on pupil outcomes?
	• Does the equipment:
	  ○ support teaching and learning?
	  ○ make staff and pupils' lives easier?
	  ○ save time?

• Dispose of/re-use any unused equipment, generating income where possible.	• Have an equipment amnesty so that all departments can dispose of unused equipment without blame. 'One man's rubbish is another man's treasure'. Any equipment which is unlikely to be used by the school can be sold, donated or properly disposed of, following the

	WEEE (Waste Electrical and Electronic Equipment) directive and regulations: http://www.hse.gov.uk/waste/waste-electrical.htm
• Negotiate value for money deals for IT equipment, taking cost and quality into account.	• Consider refurbished IT equipment/ This is becoming more popular for schools and is often high spec, in good working condition, more affordable and comes with a supplier warranty. • Have a central point for IT procurement to achieve the best deals. This will also ensure accurate asset management and strategic overview, to avoid unused equipment and/or duplicate purchases.
• Design and implement a rolling IT Refresh Programme which takes account of changes to school context, regulations and available technology.	• Your programme should be at a detailed level for the next financial year and at least outlined for the two years after that. This allows you to look ahead and be prepared for changes. The plan should be linked to your pupil number forecasts and curriculum plans and should be responsive to any significant changes. • New or changing regulations such as GDPR may have an impact on the equipment you need in school, so plan ahead to ensure that needs can be met. As each year comes to an end, another year should be outlined at the end of the plan to ensure it is continually rolling forward. • Changing technology can be difficult to keep up with. Be aware of new technologies by attending events and reading Education IT publications. Don't jump into purchasing new equipment or technology without a proper VfM assessment. Just because it is new, doesn't mean it is more suitable for your school's needs.

Are there any risks in making the changes?	How can risk be reduced or eliminated?
• Budget allocations do not allow for the level of equipment refresh needed.	• Establish a budget for IT Refresh in your multi-year budget plan. Your IT Refresh Programme should feed into your school development plan and be properly costed.
• Using older equipment creates a false economy if running costs are higher.	• Consider updating equipment earlier in your plan if it will bring cost savings in other areas, i.e. running costs.
• Purchase of new technologies or equipment do not meet school need and are not used effectively or at all.	• Try to see technology in action in a similar setting to your own. Before making a decision, speak to others who have used it rather than just suppliers. Always get an on-site demonstration or time to test before making a big purchase.

What is the expected impact of the change?

- Purchase of IT equipment and consumables is co-ordinated to ensure value for money.
- Underused equipment is either put to better use or disposed of.
- Decisions on new purchases are carefully considered, taking cost, quality and expected impact on outcomes into account.
- All new purchases are properly evaluated to inform future decisions.
- IT equipment is kept up to date, is properly accounted for and is adequately budgeted for, creating an environment where IT supports learning, makes people's lives easier and saves time without being a hindrance.

17 REVIEWING FUNCTIONAL AREAS

What are functional areas?

There are some areas of the school's operation that can be regarded as specific objectives or functions, which are more strategic in nature than the normal categories of expenditure that we have already considered. These merit an individual focus, because they are likely to be closely aligned to your educational vision.

Taking a holistic approach that looks at strategic areas will add an extra dimension to your budget review. Simply looking at the nuts and bolts of what you spend your money on, without considering specific groups of pupils or the way in which staff operate across the school, could result in an unexpected impact on key strands of your activities.

In this chapter, we show you some examples, firstly for Special Educational Needs and Disabilities (SEND) and secondly for Behaviour and Attendance. You will be able to identify other priorities and areas of activity according to your own focus or areas that need improvement as a result of inspection. Some may be funded from alternative sources such as Pupil Premium, post-16 funding or separate grants, but it is likely that your budget share will be making an additional contribution.

Some other examples, although not an exhaustive list, could be disadvantaged pupils, Looked After Children, early years, post-16, Professional Development and leadership/governor development, recruitment and retention, parental engagement, community and/or business links, or any area where there is a specific challenge. The same approach can be applied to any of these, using our template to question yourself on the issues and appropriate areas to review.

Special Educational Needs and Disabilities (SEND)

Special Educational Needs and Disabilities (SEND) is an area of activity where getting it right can make a significant difference to individual pupils, their families, staff and leaders, and the school's reputation.

As the population grows, there may also be an increase in the number of pupils with particular needs, such as autism spectrum disorder (ASD) and social, emotional and mental health (SEMH) needs. Mainstream schools may therefore be more likely to see pupils with SEND taking up places.

This may trigger a need to review approaches to teaching and learning, school organisation, professional development of classroom staff and how the school builds its relationship with parents. All this has implications for your budget and it is therefore likely you will need to turn your attention to this area in your budget review.

The school funding reforms also involve a new approach to funding for SEND - the High Needs National Funding Formula. Some local authorities will receive substantially more funding for SEND but others will receive a minimal increase of 0.5% in cash terms. The new formula is likely to be unresponsive to changes in need. This will cause local authorities that aren't benefiting from the changes to look carefully at the decision-making and financial arrangements for funding SEND in schools, as part of the High Needs review that the government has required every LA to undertake.

You may therefore find that your LA has moved money away from the pot for school budgets in order to cover High Needs pressures. If you are a very inclusive school, you might come under greater challenge from your LA to prove how you have spent the element of your budget share that's deemed to be for SEND costs before qualifying for additional funding. Alternatively, there may be a greater expectation that mainstream schools in your local area will educate more pupils with SEND, pushing thresholds higher before pupils will be deemed appropriate for specialist placements.

Our template below makes reference to this, but even if you experience the same levels of SEND as before, the budget review provides an opportunity to ensure you are as effective as possible while achieving VfM.

Budget area: Special Educational Needs and Disabilities
Why or how might waste/inefficiency occur?
• Provision is focused on individual children without considering the potential for streamlining across small groups. • Insufficient analysis of need, resulting in provision which does not adequately support pupils. • Insufficient research into options for provision to find the most cost-effective methods.

What can be done to improve efficiency?	What is the process for making this happen?
• Ensure a strategic approach to SEND.	• Ensure there is sufficient senior leadership capacity and skills to take a strategic approach to SEND. • Build relationships with key LA and Health decision-makers and become familiar with funding systems for SEND. • Develop a full understanding of the progress made by pupils with SEND and the key issues to address. • Check you are receiving all the funding you are entitled to for pupils with SEND, through a consistent dialogue with the LA SEND team. • Decide whether to supplement your notional SEN budget* with other funding from your main budget or other sources such as grants. * The notional SEN budget is an element within your school budget share which the LA deems is for SEN support. The calculation of this element varies between LAs, but the first £10k of total costs for an individual pupil should be funded from it.
• More robust analysis of children's individual needs and the most effective approaches to meet them.	• Better training for all classroom staff to help them identify needs early and make appropriate provision or referrals to obtain specialist support as required. • Purchase Education Psychology and School Improvement Adviser time (LA, MAT or external) to advise on effective approaches and the most efficient way of implementing them in your school.
• Ensure spending on SEND represents value for money.	• Map out your spending on SEND and identify any overlaps, e.g. purchase of items for individuals which could be shared in small groups, inefficient staff deployment, missed opportunities for personalisation of teaching etc.

	• Check that procurement procedures are followed when purchasing items of equipment. This could include getting the specification right to ensure the correct level of goods or services is requested and evaluating responses to achieve an appropriate balance between quality and price.
	• Check that the provision you are making for pupils with SEND is the most appropriate choice. Are you making a default assumption that the allocation of teaching assistant hours is the best approach? For a particular pupil, this could create an unhelpful dependence on another person. Providing assistive technology might have a much greater impact and suit their wish for independent learning.
	• If TA support is appropriate, do these staff have the appropriate skills, knowledge and experience for the type of need they are supporting?
Are there any risks in making the changes?	**How can risk be reduced or eliminated?**
• Insufficient expertise or willingness among staff to implement changes.	• Address professional development requirements and build SEND awareness into appraisal targets.

What is the expected impact of the change?

- The school receives SEND funding it is entitled to, enabling pupils to be properly supported.
- Value for money is achieved – SEND provision is recognised as a priority in order to support pupils to make progress in line with their potential, at an appropriate level of investment.
- Resources (staff, facilities, equipment) are used effectively and are available when needed.
- Specialist support is obtained when needed, to enhance the school's own provision.
- School teachers, leaders and governors will be able to prove to Ofsted that they are complying with the requirement to understand how SEND funding is being used to improve outcomes for relevant pupils.

Behaviour and attendance

Behaviour and attendance are key areas which can have a significant adverse impact on a school's standards of attainment and achievement. If not handled correctly, they may cause reputational damage, leading to a decline in popularity which may result in lower applications for admission. This can in turn adversely impact on the amount of funding received.

If a school prioritises early identification of pupils who are at risk of exclusion or poor attendance, and establishes capacity, skills and systems to provide the right type and level of support, it will be in control of its culture.

On the other hand, if problems are allowed to escalate, the school will be forced to react to events, which can represent a major distraction from teaching and learning as well as creating an unpleasant environment for pupils and staff alike. The school will also face significant challenges in inspection if it is evident that behaviour and attendance are poor.

It is therefore better to incur lower costs on building the foundations for pastoral care and early support than to face high costs for specialist interventions.

Budget area: Behaviour and Attendance
Why or how might waste/inefficiency occur?
• Failure to address challenging behaviour at an early stage results in significant staff resource being taken up in managing pupils in crisis, with the potential for escalation and disruption to a wider group of learners. If this is not handled well, the school can attract unwelcome attention which could affect parental views and future admissions, causing a drop in funding.
• If pupils have to be excluded, the school will face a clawback of funding which could have been used to allow them to re-engage in learning.
• Poor attendance can require additional staffing, both in teaching time to enable absentees to catch up and in attendance officer time for interventions. There will also be an impact on administrative staff, who will have to engage in administrative processes leading up to formal action such as penalty notices and evidence to the LA for court action.

What can be done to improve efficiency?	What is the process for making this happen?
• Tackle behavioural issues at source through careful	• Ensure the school development plan and budget contain actions and funding allocated for early intervention and

assessment of the root causes, such as the pupil's domestic situation, appropriateness of the curriculum/need for personalised learning, and vulnerability (e.g. bullying, mental health, substance misuse etc.).	prevention, so that pupils can be identified and supported at the earliest possible stage. • Build relationships with key LA and Health decision-makers and become familiar with available services and ways of making referrals for support, e.g. social care, health and voluntary and community organisations offering interventions, and alternative provision. • Develop a full understanding of the progress made by pupils with challenging behaviour and the key issues to address. • Monitor performance in terms of sanctions and the level of fixed term and permanent exclusions, to determine the effectiveness of interventions and act on your findings.
• Tackle poor attendance to ensure that prompt action is taken to achieve improvements, ensuring that teachers are not put under pressure by having to help absentees to catch up.	• Assess the capacity needed to tackle poor attendance, and decide whether to organise in-house support or buy in services from elsewhere. • Ensure that there is regular reporting to senior leaders and governors to allow them to monitor attendance, evaluate the effectiveness of interventions and act on the findings.
• Ensure that spending on alternative provision represents value for money.	• Check that you have full information about the most appropriate alternative provision to prevent exclusion, to assess whether it will meet the needs of pupils for whom the school's interventions have not worked. Check if the LA has any information about approved providers. • Ensure that you have a formal agreement with AP providers with whom you place pupils, outlining their responsibilities. This will help to maximise the outcomes for pupils

	who remain on your roll and achieve clarity over what you are paying for. • Ensure that pupil progress is discussed regularly with the AP provider and take action if it is not satisfactory.
Are there any risks in making the changes?	**How can risk be reduced or eliminated?**
• Insufficient expertise or willingness among staff to implement changes.	• Address professional development requirements and build awareness of behaviour and attendance into appraisal targets.

• Poor local choice of Alternative Provision to support early intervention and prevent exclusion, for example:
  o not enough options exist;
  o costs are unreasonable;
  o it does not achieve the desired outcomes for pupils on your roll who are attending for a short intervention or on a part time basis.
	• Engage support from other schools in opening up discussions with the LA to stimulate the market and put proper quality assurance in place.
	• Talk to other schools, trusts and MATs in your local area to explore the potential for setting up shared early intervention provision.
	• Look at provision in neighbouring areas, while considering the cost of transport and the potential barriers to attendance that this may represent.
	• Check that you are complying with statutory guidance by:
	  o drawing up a specification for the provision you need before commissioning it
	  o satisfying yourself that it is suitable for the learner at an individual level
	  o carrying out your monitoring responsibilities effectively for commissioned provision
	  o challenging and addressing any shortcomings in the providers' offer.

What is the expected impact of the change?

- The school identifies pupils at risk of exclusion at an early stage, enabling them to be assessed and properly supported so that their needs are met. This will prevent too much teaching time being spent on pupils in crisis.
- Value for money is achieved when pupils are sent to AP to re-engage in learning, with improved outcomes being achieved at a reasonable cost.
- The school's funding is spent on prevention and early intervention which gives pupils a better chance of success, rather than on clawback of funding for exclusions, which represents an unproductive use of resources.
- Direct action using pastoral staff reduces absence at a low cost to the school, compared to the cost of extra teaching costs to enable persistent absentees to catch up on missed work and the diversion of administrative staff to handle processes for punitive actions.

Part 4: Finalising Your Review

18 FORECASTING AND MONITORING IMPACT

Financial savings and other benefits

The impact of a budget review should largely be in terms of financial savings, although there may be other positive impacts such as savings in staff time, better work-life balance and improved staff well-being. If you have worked through all the cultural changes in a careful and considered manner, the risk of negative impact should have been managed and minimised and the benefits should outweigh the costs.

It is the role of the budget review leader to coordinate the forecasting and monitoring of financial savings, although teams will contribute to this by offering their judgements and estimates in relation to their own areas.

The budget review leader should work with each team to estimate financial savings. As far as possible, this should be based on data which leads to a professional judgement, rather than a wild guess. That is not to say that forecasting will be accurate at this stage; a large amount of guesswork will be involved, but basing estimates on knowledge, data and expertise is the preferred approach.

In coordinating information from each team, watch out for duplication of ideas or solutions between areas. Make sure that two teams don't claim the same saving when providing estimates for you to build into the budget; a saving can only be made once.

The budget review leader must also ensure they stay abreast of the overall school context. A budget review can take a long time, up to a year or even longer. Has the target for overall financial savings altered since the budget review journey began? Has the school's financial position changed significantly, for better or worse? Do changes need to be made to the budget review strategy part way through the journey?

The best way for the budget review leader to lead strategically and keep in touch with the bigger picture is to be in regular communication with the highest leadership of the school, the Headteacher and/or Executive Headteacher and School Business Leader or Finance Director (if this is not their role).

This knowledge is extremely important for two reasons. If the level of savings required increases, the budget review leader may find themselves needing to revisit particular budgets to attempt to increase savings further still. If the requirement for savings reduces, this may avoid a compromising decision which could have led to a less than favourable impact on pupil outcomes.

Building savings into the budget

When you have established the level of savings you think you can expect, you need to consider how you should show these in future years' budgets, if at all.

You need to ask yourself what is the likelihood of these savings being achieved. If you do judge it as a low risk to show future year budgets at a reduced level, be transparent with your explanations and note in your budget planning documents what action is needed, and what success it relies on, to become a reality.

Set out clear monitoring processes to make sure the forecasted savings are achieved. The finance team should support you with this and provide information, at least monthly, to enable early intervention if it becomes apparent that savings may not be realised. Remember that savings can arise from reduced spending or increased income generation.

Finally, how will the estimated savings impact on outcomes? What will you be able to do now that you couldn't do before this review? The answer to this question will depend on the over-arching objective you set at the beginning of the review.

If the purpose of this review is to avoid a deficit or support a deficit recovery plan, then you shouldn't be planning to spend the savings on other things. Ensure your deficit recovery plan is regularly updated so that you have a clear picture of the remaining challenge ahead.

If, however, your purpose was to achieve savings that could then be used to fund other school improvement initiatives, have you saved enough to be able to do this and what will the expected impact of the new initiative be on pupil outcomes? You will need to regularly revisit your balances plan (or reserves target) to ensure this is up to date and is effectively informing your future spending decisions in order to achieve the maximum impact on pupil outcomes.

Whichever circumstances you are working in, it is important to keep testing the validity of your financial plans. Identify risks and mitigating actions to make sure you can achieve a balanced budget or target level of reserves, meeting any criteria or conditions set by your funding body.

Keep a record in your strategic action plan of all of your reflections for financial forecasting and monitoring the impact of your budget review. Remember that this is a working document which should be added to at every stage of the process, to ensure a complete record of every aspect of your review.

19 KEEPING STAKEHOLDERS INFORMED

Reporting to governors

Your strategic action plan, with accompanying notes, will be of particular use when you report to governors.

This is an essential part of the process to enable governors to hold school leaders to account and be fully informed about the school's financial strategy. Governors are responsible for ensuring the school's financial health and the budget review is a critical exercise in achieving this.

You are likely to produce a report specifically written for your governing board to inform them and update them of the purpose, approach and progress of the budget review. This may be less detailed than the strategic action plan itself, giving more of a big picture view of the work that has been undertaken. Your strategic action plan and accompanying notes form an internal working document, but will act as a useful aide-memoire when answering any questions from governors as they appropriately challenge the process to gain a deeper understanding.

Ensure minutes of governing board meetings are sufficiently detailed, enclosing copies of the reports and presentations made, as well as the questions and challenge from governors and the responses from school leaders. These minutes, the report presented to governors, the strategic action plan, the budget plans and the financial monitoring reports all combine to create a useful collection of evidence. Appropriate elements of this can be used to give reassurances on your school's financial health to a number of stakeholders, including your funding body, the DfE, existing or potential future partners and unions.

Stakeholder interests

Your funding body - either the LA or the ESFA - and the DfE may require evidence that action has been undertaken to resolve or prevent a deficit situation.

Existing or potential partners may need reassurance that the school is a valid going concern and that it is beneficial to them to continue working with, or start to work with, the school on a formal basis. This will be of particular importance if you are looking to join a Multi-Academy Trust (MAT). The Trust will need to carry out a due diligence exercise to ensure it is in their interest to work with you and ensure it is not beyond their own realistic financial capacity.

If you are embarking on a financially-driven staffing reduction exercise, unions may require evidence and reassurance that the school has undertaken all possible solutions to avoid compulsory redundancy. Whilst it is not essential to produce a formal budget review for this purpose, it can be a very powerful trail of evidence to prove this very point when the school has no other option left but to reduce staffing.

20 CONCLUSION

Reflections

We hope that this book has been helpful in demonstrating how to lead a budget review, and that it has deepened your understanding of the important threads that need to be woven together to make your budget review successful.

A budget review can help to secure a sustainable budget for your school. The value to the whole school community should not be underestimated. It can ensure the school remains a financially sound and valid entity for the future, it can protect employment if circumstances allow, and it supports the quality of education provision to maximise pupil outcomes.

In addition, a budget review can raise your profile as a leader. If necessary you can proactively raise the idea yourself, or, if it is already being discussed, you should now have the knowledge and tools you need to put yourself forward to lead the budget review with confidence.

This is an opportunity to demonstrate your ability to lead teams, lead and manage cultural and procedural change, think strategically, plan and organise, monitor and evaluate and inspire creative solutions for improvements across all aspects of school life.

The impact of a successful budget review on the school's overall capacity to achieve the priorities within its school development plan is substantial and could mean the difference between a school surviving and thriving. Leading the budget review puts you at the forefront of that success. If this is something you are given the opportunity to lead in your school, consider including your leadership of the review as an appraisal objective to demonstrate formally your development and achievements in this area.

We have provided you with practical advice for strategic and detailed action planning, offering a strong outline for your review. The running themes of risk management, cultural and procedural change management and communication will guide the implementation of your review to ensure success.

Specific examples of budget reviews for key areas provide a useful starting point, to be contextualised to your own school setting.

Reporting your budget review to key stakeholders, staff, governors, funding body, partners and unions gives others confidence in your ability to be proactive in responding to financial challenges and to secure a viable future for the school. The approach you take to reporting and communication will help you to manage expectations, keep stakeholders involved and avoid misunderstandings throughout the process.

A budget review is always good practice, but in financially uncertain and challenging times it can become an essential strategy for every school, to ensure efficiency and build a value for money culture that permeates all aspects of school life. The challenges we face as schools will get harder. By allowing us to guide you through them, you are already on the journey to overcoming those challenges. We wish you every success in your journey.

APPENDIX 1

Example of a timeline for staff review consultation process

September to December	School leaders review staffing structures and make the decision to enter into a staff review consultation, with a plan to implement staffing reductions. Advice is sought from relevant sources (HR provider, Legal support). Relevant documentation is prepared.
January/February	Consultation with staff begins. Trade union involvement in process and support offered to members throughout process.
Consultation period: (30 days/45 days/etc)	Consultation period can differ depending on local policy.
By 31st May	Notice given to staff. For teaching staff this would result in an employment end date of 31 August.

APPENDIX 2

Goleman's six leadership styles

Style	Description	Impact of Style	When to Use
Affiliative	People come first	Creates harmony and builds emotional bonds	To heal rifts in a team. To motivate people during stressful circumstances.
Authoritative	Come with me	Mobilises people towards a vision	When changes need a new vision. When a clear direction is needed.
Coaching	Try this	Develops people for the future	To help an employee improve performance. To develop long-term strengths.
Democratic	What do you think?	Forges consensus through participation	To build buy-in or consensus. To get input from valuable employees.
Pace-setting	Do as I do	Sets high standards for performance	To get quick results from a highly motivated and competent team.
Coercive	Do what I tell you	Demands immediate compliance	In a crisis. To kick-start a turnaround. With problem employees.

KEEP IN TOUCH

Thank you for reading the book; we hope you found it useful.

To continue working with us for further guidance and to share your experiences with other readers who are on that same journey, we invite you to:

- Visit our website https://schoolfinancialsuccess.com where you can:
  - Sign up to our email list to receive free regular school funding news updates, notification of blog posts and analysis of complex school funding information;
  - Read our regular blog posts on relevant topics;
  - Use the Contact Form to submit comments and ask questions.
- Visit our Facebook page @SchoolFinancialSuccess
- Follow us on Twitter at JulieCordiner_SFS: @juliecordiner

Please leave a review

We welcome feedback and would be very grateful if you could spare a moment to leave a review. It will help us to make future editions of our books better for all readers and it will also help to make it visible to other leaders and governors who may benefit from it.

Please go to the webpage where you purchased the book and let us know if we've helped you!

School Financial Success Publications

For a list of our current and planned books, please visit our website: https://schoolfinancialsuccess.com/books/. We are also building a list of topics for future books which you will find on the site; please let us know if there is a subject you would particularly like us to cover.

The first book in our School Funding Guides series is:

School Budget Mastery

Changes in school funding and rising costs are making many schools and academies anxious about their future financial position. Creating a realistic budget and keeping to it are fundamental to strong financial leadership and essential for your school's survival. 'School Budget Mastery' provides a comprehensive guide to help you achieve your goals, taking you step by step through the process of preparing your budget and monitoring progress against it throughout the year.

You will also find a wide range of advice on legal requirements, sources of funding and income, the key information needed when preparing your budget and ways to foster a positive financial culture in your school at all levels. With our guidance, you can achieve value for money and a prudent, effective approach to the use of resources.

Suitable for all school leaders, in particular practising and aspiring Headteachers, SBLs, governors and others with a role or interest in school finance, this book will help you to grow in confidence and achieve financial success for your school.

"A really informative and useful guide to all aspects of school and academy budgeting, relevant for both finance professionals and teachers with leadership responsibilities" Jim Farquhar, MAT Director of Finance & Corporate Services.

ABOUT THE AUTHORS

Julie Cordiner
Education Funding Specialist

I'm a qualified accountant and independent consultant specialising in school funding and education finance, with over thirty years experience in local authority education work including ten years as an Assistant Director. Between 2007 and 2015 I was a member of DfE's advisory group on school funding. I advise schools and local authorities on school funding and achieving value for money in order to support better outcomes and enable children and young people to maximise their potential, something I'm passionate about. Everyone deserves the best possible education and we all need to use taxpayers' money wisely, to achieve a fair chance for every single pupil.

Nikola Flint
School Business Leader

With a background in accountancy and sixteen years experience in the school business management profession, I fulfil a broad, strategic role as Director of Corporate Services in a large secondary school leading on all aspects of school organisation and SMSC. My experience as a Specialist Leader of Education offering school to school support has widened my perspective of the challenges faced by schools and the potential solutions to those challenges. I passionately believe that every child has the right to a high quality education and that we all have a part to play in achieving this ideal.

NOTES

NOTES

NOTES

NOTES

NOTES

Printed in Great Britain
by Amazon

47871491R00086